THE ELUSIVE IDEAL OF COMMUNITY

By Geoff Beech

Lifeworld Education
6 Kalimna Close
LAKE HAVEN 2263
AUSTRALIA

Email: geoff@lifeworldeducation.com

ISBN 978-1-63625-478-4

Unless otherwise noted, the Scripture quotations in this publication are from the New International Version (NIV) of the Bible

Cover Design: 'Community' by Tiffany Chavez

This book is dedicated
to my wonderful advisor,
sounding board, and companion:
my wife,
Dr Elizabeth Beech

Table of Contents

1. Introduction

"How good and pleasant it is when God's people live together in unity!" (Psalm 133:1)

As image-bearers of the triune God, we are essentially communal, a fact that Western scholars in particular frequently overlook. We were created to live in community with God and with others, a fact that Eastern Christians, who live in a culture that emphasizes personal responsibilities toward the group more than rugged individualism, understand well.[1]

H uman relationality is a foundational feature of our existence. In addition to contributing to our feelings of well-being, it has even been demonstrated to have a very significant influence on our physical health. Christian institutions, organisations, or groups, of all types, consist of human beings congregating, face-to-face or virtually, for specific purposes. As Christians, we work towards creating and sustaining 'community', and this may be done for a range of reasons. It may be in order to promote a sense of order, cohesion, peace, fraternity, safety, or a bonding of some type, but, as we are relational beings, it may be because we simply seek to be a part of a space where we can relate to others. The desire for community, for whatever reason, is evident in the quantity of literature the topic has stimulated. Since the beginning of the millennium, the WorldCat publishing database records a doubling of the book titles published each year that include the word community, and in recent years, the number has been almost a quarter of a million each year. This seeking to understand the idea of community, or desiring a sense, or a feeling, of community, has been complicated recently by the isolating conditions often demanded by the COVID-19 pandemic. Perhaps, then, it is not so much that we want 'community', but our emotional selves seek, often with some urgency, the cozy feeling of non-threatening connectedness with others.

Nothing and no one can stand in isolation. Everything (and everyone) is connected with other things, with other people, and with the past. Within the context of human beings living in community, however, a great deal of confusion exists. This book considers the task of putting relationality perhaps in something of a different perspective. Hopefully, it will provide a starting point for thinking about how we relate and what that means for individuals within groups, and the implications this may have

---

[1] Gould, 2019, p. 28

for leaders of groups. While much of the material in this book may seem obvious to many of us, there are some sections that the reader may not have considered. The intention is to raise awareness of a range of fairly common relationship structures so that group members and leaders can identify the type of structure of a group, or the structure from which a group member may have come, and therefore be given clues as to how and why individuals relate and the implications these have on actions and reactions.

There are so many dimensions across which cultures may be measured or categorized but one of the most commonly referenced is the idea of community. Community membership, however, is a very broad term. When we speak, for example, of a Christian school as a 'community' we think in terms of the students, staff, board members, and any others who may be stakeholders in the institution's activities. Regarding the Church, N. T. Wright has said that God has provided for human beings, "a network of worship-based, rigorous, egalitarian, philanthropic, fictive, kinship groups."[2] In other words, he provided a Church. Within a local church context, what we call community usually refers to the congregation and those who serve it. In addition to the definition of membership, what is inferred in the use of the term 'Church community' is the wide range of interconnections—the relationships of different types that exist (or we might wish existed) for various purposes between 'community' members. All community members are always seen in terms of relationships. Yet, of course, this is complicated in that within any such community, not only will each individual be unique, but the relationship each has with any other member, and to all members as a group, will also be unique. The sociation of complex human beings is necessarily complicated but also relationships constantly morph and evolve over time, adding exponentially to the complexity.

Examples are provided in later chapters of interpersonal relationships that are seen through the Scriptures, where people are seen in terms of being *homo socialis*: bound, often tightly, to specific groups. Apart from biblical hints, today, of course, we all have our varied understandings of the word *community* and we use it frequently, but we might also remember that our definitions have been colored by our individualistic, Western ways of seeing reality. According to the Online Etymological Dictionary, the origin of the word community in the late 14th century related to people being associated together because they resided in the same locality, with connotations later of the common people and also linked to land held in common. The various current definitions of the word 'community' involve some form of sharing: shared history, shared resources, shared beliefs, shared practices, and so on. As with all of our language, the way we understand the term is through the lenses provided by our culture as meaning is

---

[2] N. T. Wright, 2018

developed with others as we create and learn meaning together. We, in the West in the 21st century, therefore have a very particular view of what community might mean but that does not mean that all people of all times have held the same view.

In the rest of this chapter, we will consider a little of the background to studies of human interrelatedness as well as points, in a notional series of relationship categories that form a simple typology. As we consider the components of this series, we will also see examples from Western and other cultures. Not all cultures view relationships in the same way or for the same purposes. For those working in education, this provides some useful background on topics we may want to explore in greater depth—either because we have students from different cultures in our classes, because we present papers for those in different cultures, or because, as Christian educators, we wish to live in Godly relationships with our students and peers. For those involved with church ministries, the impacts of globalisation and immigration mean that a range of cultures and, therefore, relationship structures may be present in a congregation. Understanding the breadth of these relationship structures and their implications is important, not only for interpersonal relationships but also for issues of trust and its consequences for knowledge theory, as well as teaching and learning. Thoughtful application of the ideas surrounding the development of a biblically grounded 'community' is not only for our benefit, but for all group members.

There are many variants of the claim: "Give me a child until he is seven and I will show you the man." These include versions attributed to Aristotle, Vladimir Ilyich Lenin ("Give me four years to teach the children and the seed I have sown will never be uprooted"), and, of course we have the biblical principle, "Train up a child in the way he should go: and when he is old, he will not depart from it" (Proverbs 22:6). To disciple students or church congregation members to become Godly members of the school, college, or church, becomes a significant purpose for us. This discipling is founded on a common understanding of 'meaning' for a very wide range of things and that 'meaning', as mentioned, is developed together in relationship. It would seem to follow therefore that the stronger the 'community' the stronger the acquired 'meaning' of whatever is taught or discussed.

In Scripture, the Divine admonition was that Fallen human beings seek redemption in a context of feeling and expressing some form of love for each other. From the Middle Ages, sociologists, anthropologists, philosophers, theologians, and political scientists have attempted to understand human relationships and develop some structures so that there may be co-existence for mutual benefit. For many, the relationship structures, however, were not necessarily loving. We see, for example, the enforced structures promoted in Machiavelli's concern with ultimate power in *The Prince* in 1513, and also Nietzsche's recognition of the human will to power—a power relationship over others. Another vision of humanity that has social implications is that of Hobbes, who, writing in *Leviathan* in 1651, saw human beings in mechanistic terms, noting that the behaviour of humans may be explained in terms of robotics: our hearts being springs, our nerves, strings, our joints, wheels, and so on. When Hobbes' conceptualisation is transferred to society as a whole, human interactions are seen merely in terms of utilitarian social contracts. A contractual basis for relationships and the rights and obligations of citizenry is seen later in John Locke's *Second Treatise of Government*, and Jean-Jacques Rousseau's 18th-century work, *The Social Contract.* Apart from the political and state structures, the interactions between individuals were seen in these Enlightenment writings as primarily transactional, involving exchange and reciprocity as individuals sociated for mutual benefit. The works of the humanist-oriented philosophers, however, still begged the question of how human beings might live together if all religious or traditional justifications for authority were no longer valued and therefore neither effective nor persuasive.

Utilitarian social contracts aside, the fundamental human need is to sociate, to be in relationship and to be included by others. Indeed, Stuart Fowler indicated the importance of association for the 'self', saying: "The human person finds self-fulfilment only as life is directed towards a source of meaning beyond itself, whether as individual or as communal self"[3] (c.f., the biblical idea of *agape*, giving love). The importance of sociation was also reflected in Abraham Maslow's famous *Hierarchy of Needs*, where he noted the significance of belonging and a hunger for human interaction.

> I believe that the tremendous and rapid increase in T-groups [therapy groups] and other personal growth groups and intentional communities may in part be motivated by this unsatisfied hunger for contact, for intimacy, for belongingness and by the need to overcome the widespread feelings of alienation, aloneness, strangeness, and loneliness, which have been worsened by our mobility, by the breakdown of traditional groupings, the scattering of families, the generation gap, the steady urbanization and disappearance of village face-to-faceness, and the resulting shallowness of American friendship. My strong impression is also that some proportion of youth rebellion groups—I don't know how many or how much—is motivated by the profound hunger for groupiness, for contact, for real togetherness in the face of a common enemy, any enemy that can serve to form an amity group simply by posing an external threat. The same kind of thing was observed in groups of soldiers who were pushed into an unwanted brotherliness and intimacy by their common external danger, and who may stick together

---

[3] Fowler, 1993, p. 24

throughout a lifetime as a consequence. Any good society must satisfy this need, one way or another, if it is to survive and be healthy.[4]

Perhaps it has been the increasing diminution of groupiness in our increasingly digitized Western society that has led to the proliferation of concerned literature on the theme. The demise of solidarity in the developed world today has been bemoaned by some who have commented on the loss of the shared values that form the cement of human society. The root cause of this phenomenon is claimed to lie in the desire to monetize everything, as well as the institutionalization of individualism. The way self-esteem may be monetized acts as a filter for our relationships and weakens them. At the same time, there has been the continuing rise of some forms of elective community, such as sporting associations, as well as the virtual communities provided by social media. As Jenny Anderson and many others have commented, however, the latter usually lack substance.

> Thanks to Facebook and Instagram, many of us are still nominally in touch with our high-school friends and co-workers from several jobs ago. But in our daily lives, communities are shrinking. From 1985 to 2009, the average size of an American's social network—defined by the number of confidants people feel they have—has declined by more than one-third. We may have hundreds of friends on Instagram, but evidence is mounting that those connections are not the ones that provide us the social balm we need, which is human contact. Instead, the more "connected" we become, the more we seem to let our social relationships atrophy, failing to catch up with an old friend, invite a neighbor over for coffee, or engage in some of life's banal daily rituals—talking with someone on the way to the tube, getting coffee from a cafe where you know the barista's name—which soothe our social needs.[5]

A further clarification

Many authors use terms relating to community and society, interchangeably. This is not helpful if one is to try to locate a particular understanding, or develop a typology, in order to examine it with the intention of bringing some form of improvement to human situations. For the states of relationship we will consider in the following chapters, *society, community, collective,* and *commune*, should all be seen not so much as degrees of relatedness where there is a perceived need to move from one to another. Rather, each is a *framework* within which human beings will relate to each other in a particular range of ways, often inhabiting a number, even at the same time, but usually with one dominating. Relationships within each will also vary in intensity, as dictated by

---

[4] Maslow, 1970, p. 44
[5] Anderson, 2019, para. 10

personal choice, pragmatics, or obligation. Each will also exhibit expressions of, and definitions of, interpersonal relationships, such as mere social contact, friendship, brotherly love, *agape* love, and so on. Each will be exercised according to its appropriateness for the group's particular structure and function. Each type of grouping provides a *structure* that is influenced by some *pragmatic goals* and by members having *something in common*, including, in varying degrees, sharing a *history, context, purpose*, and *value set*. It also includes interpersonal communications and communication structures or protocols. At its most basic level, such communication includes the identification of the self to others as a member of the group and, therefore, presumably, one's agreement with commonly held beliefs and practices of the group, or at least the desire to do so. In our daily living, we do not stop to think about how each works as we move from one to another; we simply 'know' intuitively and adapt accordingly.

Worldview assumptions

Before proceeding, it is worth reflecting briefly on the idea of the worldview assumptions we all hold at a pretheoretical, or preconscious, level and how these influence relationality. There are many books and articles on this topic, but for the moment, it is only necessary that we think of them as being largely subconscious 'beliefs' that are linked to our surroundings and culture, and that can control our stated beliefs and actions. In particular, in the context of this book, we should recognise that these strongly influence the way we see interpersonal relationships and guide our navigation through them. If we have not lived in or observed other cultures and their operational relationships, it may be difficult to see our own. (The last thing a fish discovers is water!) They are strongly linked to culture and are what Charles Taylor referred to as the "social imaginary" that culture members have. A lack of cross-cultural contexts, and therefore a lack of referential comparisons, may limit our understanding of the relationality that God has built into us as His image bearers. For this reason, a range of cultural insights is given later in this book to help us comprehend the depth of some different relationship constructs. This understanding is important, as is the ability to articulate types of relationships within our institutional and theological contexts.

Perhaps we should note that for most of us, the idea of understanding another culture is not considered to be particularly difficult. Yet, most of our understanding, either through travel, reading, or casual contact, is at a very superficial level. An illustration given by Kenneth Bailey, however, shows some of the depth that may be involved:

> I can recall vividly, in the village of Kom al-Akhdar in the south of Egypt, asking a particular person about the village traditions. He was in his sixties

and seemed to be an appropriate person to ask. He offered a few remarks and
was soon interrupted by others around the circle who said,

"He wouldn't understand—he is not from this village."

"How long has he lived here?" I queried.

"Only thirty-seven years," came the calm answer.[6]

Of course, learning another language so that one is very fluent is a help, as
language and culture are very closely linked. Some of the difficulties this poses are
seen in various places in this book where we consider the language and culture of the
characters in the Old and New Testaments, as well as in other cultures. Hopefully,
however, the insights given will be useful for our everyday encounters with others.

That said, this book is not a sociology—there are many books and articles written
in that vein—though the nature of the topic here implies sociological perspectives.
Rather, it is an exploration of what Donati and Archer described as 'organisational
man'—human beings as individuals in a range of contexts organising themselves and
inter-relating for different reasons. These ways may be conceptualised in the
hypothetical series related to relationality as follows.

A relationship series

> NOTE: The inclusion of this relationship series, and its components described
> here and in the following chapters, is not to provide a complete 'how to' for
> handling relationships in organisations and institutions. Rather, the idea is to
> provide some background frameworks that may be helpful in thinking through
> relationship issues using different tools—some from sociology and some from
> anthropology. In some ways, this book may be seen, then, perhaps in terms
> of being a starting point, rather than a conclusion to the subject.

For human beings, the essentialness of relationship follows the Scriptural
descriptions of co-existence as members of one body (Ephesians 4), branches of a
vine (John 15), or a temple constructed of living stones (1 Peter 2), and so on. One
means proposed here is through a typology in the form of a series signifying different
relational or interrelational strengths, purposes, and qualities. Lonner and Berry
suggested that the concepts of individualism and collectivism seem to appear as
endpoints of a continuum and noted that this may form a useful way to examine the
variability of human interactions. For our purposes here, we propose an extension of
this concept. Each category in the series has particular characteristics, and the
members of each have more-or-less defined rules for engagement with others, as well

---

[6] Bailey, 1991, p. 39

as limitations on inter-member trust, and the attending implications regarding the defining of truth (epistemology). The series items are not quantised and exhibit very blurred boundaries at times, so that all individuals or groups of individuals will exhibit a range of relationships, though they will be prioritised to a particular category based on culture, personality, worldview, and temporal contexts. For the purposes of this work, where a particular emphasis is placed on community, collectivity and communality, we may summarise the relationship categories as follows:

- Individual
- Society
- Community
- Collective
- Commune
- New Creation/Earth
- Perichoresis

In ascending order, each category implies a distinct way of relating at greater depth compared with the previous one. Apart from the New Creation/Earth (as far as we know) and, of course, Perichoresis, the interrelatedness of the Trinity, this also implies different ways of understanding the teaching and learning tasks that are so central to education and also important in church life. Understanding the emphasis, or priority, given within any group of human beings to one of these categories assists us in communicating cross-culturally, but also is useful in terms of the consideration given to particular aspects of our own institutions. The series categories cannot be mapped directly to cultures or institutions, though, in very general terms, Western cultures tend to promote individuality, many Latin, Middle Eastern and Asian cultures exhibit forms of collectivity, and cultures based on small groups, such as tribes or small villages, may promote forms of communality. For us to try to force other cultures to relate as we do is, of course, imperialistic, but this is the way colonising cultures have functioned for centuries. Instead, we may learn much from the relational structures that are seen as priorities in other cultures—especially as these will exist to at least some extent in our own, and often may be more biblical. In particular, we may see more clearly the "*I*" culture in which we live in the West and compare it with the communal sharing, decision-making and ownership of another culture.

Given our lack of knowledge and the themes of this book, New Creation/Earth relationships and Perichoresis will not be considered in any depth, but the other categories have been well studied in practice by many. For our purposes, -ism terms will be used frequently. While the use of this suffix refers to belief systems or ideologies, a distinction must be made between ideology and experienced affiliations. The suffixed terms are useful in order to define and highlight the features of the categories when taken to an extreme, or at least where the particular relationship state is considered to be 'normal' or 'just the way things are', hence: individualism, societism, communitarianism, collectivism, and communalism. That said, a source of considerable confusion is the wide range of definitions commonly given to each of the relationship terms—not only by different authors, but often an author will use two or more of the terms (particularly society, community, collectivity, and communality) interchangeably. Through this book, an effort has been made to try to limit interchangeability as much as possible by giving specific definitions, though we will see that in quotations, other authors do not.

When it comes to a relationship series, a range of formats also exists. Many researchers have compared Western and Eastern, or Western and Latin people groups and therefore have concentrated on the individualism-collectivism dichotomy as one of the fundamental defining characteristics of cultures. The studies have been based on these major cultural types and do not consider community or communitarianism as that, for them, does not appear to be a culture-defining concept. While we may make further distinctions, Moemeka and others have suggested a three-component continuum based on the three major cultural types: Individualism, Collectivism, and Communalism. The defining features of these he claimed, are as follows, using categories commonly found in research works by Geert Hofstede, Harry Triandis, Robert House, and others:

INDIVIDUALISM
- Universalistic
- Self-interest
- Self-reliant
- Achievement-oriented
- Individual rights
- Low-context communication

COLLECTIVISM
- Universalistic
- Group-individual interest
- Cooperation
- Achievement-oriented
- Collective-individual welfare
- Low-context communication

COMMUNALISM
- Particularistic

- Communal interest
- Coordination
- Ascription-oriented
- Community welfare
- High-context communication[7]

For Moemeka the other extreme on the continuum from individualism is not collectivism but communalism, a type of social order where one is encouraged, or forced, to lose oneself for the welfare of the group. It is this continuum between, and including, these two 'extremes' of individualism and communalism that the following chapters attempt to address in more depth. To conclude this introductory chapter, however, some very brief words on the 'outliers' from the series: New Creation or New Earth relationships and the relationships that may exist between the members of the Triune Godhead—Father, Son and Holy Spirit.

New Creation, or New Earth, and Perichoresis

> However, as it is written: 'What no eye has seen, what no ear has heard, and what no human mind has conceived'—the things God has prepared for those who love Him. (1 Corinthians 2:9)

Little may be said here regarding both the relationships anticipated in the New Earth and regarding Perichoresis. There are areas of speculation for us in the now-but-not-yet in which we find ourselves, and with the severe limitations placed on us as finite human beings. The Scriptures give only general hints, and given our finitude, that is probably all that we can absorb. Also, these are areas more pertinent to treatment by theologians rather than educators, sociologists, or philosophers.

The hints as to what form the New Earth relationships may take are found primarily in Isaiah 11 and 65, Revelation 21, and 2 Peter 3. The most notable thing we see in these passages is that the relationship structures we now know will be broken down in a new order. We may presume, however, that the greed, pride, power seeking, and lack of trust inherent in individualism and the adversarial nature of collectivism will be no more. The governing principle of love will be brought to complete fulfilment, and it is difficult for us at the moment to grasp the wonder of that reality. But we will know, and presumably we will learn. "For now we see only a reflection as in a mirror; then we shall see face to face. Now I know in part; then I shall know fully, even as I am fully known"

---

[7] Moemeka, 1998, p. 126

(1 Corinthians 13:12). Truth perception, unencumbered by fallen natures, will be complete in ways we cannot imagine. Presumably echoing Plato's *simulacrum*, the 19th-century theologian, John Henry Newman, requested the epitaph inscription on his tombstone to be: "*Ex umbris et imaginibus in veritatem*" (From the shadows and images to the truth).

Perichoresis

As mentioned, Perichoresis is a topic for a theological paper, but in the relationship series model, it may be seen as lying not simply far beyond individualism, societism, communitarianism, collectivism, communalism, and New Earth/Heaven relationships, but *infinitely* so. We cannot imagine the depth of the relationship between the members of our Triune God. Their *amor infinitus* love and omniscience are beyond our grasp and forever will be.

The bottom line

In the following chapters, as we consider each of the series categories individually, we will see the difficulty of developing genuine Christian community within each of the structures in which we are placed and within which we relate to each other.

Following a general discussion on human relatedness, the following chapters of the book cover a series of points in a little more depth. Below is a brief summary of them in terms of their '-isms'. As we are very familiar with individuals, societies and communities, more space has been allocated to collectivities and communes.

- Individualism (Chapter 3) is the lens through which Western cultures view human beings. We are seen as independent and having agency to think and act without necessary reference to others.

- Societism (Chapter 4) sees human beings brought formally or informally into what is usually a superficial relationship for specific, utilitarian purposes.

- Communitarianism (Chapter 5) sees humans sociating freely under common values, beliefs, or purposes, but there may be a depth of relationship between community members and freedom to interact in a range of ways.

- Collectivism (Chapter 6), while evident in most Western groups, is even more evident in non-Western cultures such as those of Latin America, Asia and the Middle East. Adherence to an ingroup core and rejection of outgroups are significant features of collectivism.

- Communalism (Chapters 7 & 8) connotes a much deeper level of interpersonal relationship for significant reasons, and frequently, such a depth may only be gained by being born into the group. Some of the forms of communality that are discussed include Christian and non-Christian, voluntary and forced, living in communes and in tribal or small village groups.

2. Human Relatedness

"Life in its true sense is a relationship."[1]

Whoever does not love does not know God, because God is love. No one has ever seen God; but if we love one another, God lives in us and His love is made complete in us. Whoever claims to love God yet hates a brother or sister is a liar. For whoever does not love their brother and sister, whom they have seen, cannot love God, whom they have not seen. (1 John 4: 8, 12, 20)

Before we consider the individual components of our relationship series, we might ruminate a little on human relationality. This is an extremely broad topic and our considerations will only be brief, picking out some salient points and leaving readers to complete their own picture from personal knowledge, their own reading, and experience. In the previous chapter, mention was made of Abraham Maslow's view of interpersonal relationships and the human need to belong and feel that we belong. We all prefer to exist in stable interpersonal relationships. At times, we may make a very considerable effort to protect and enhance our interconnectedness with others and resist relationship dissolution with its attendant psychological and perhaps physical suffering. This need for the love and respect given to us by others appears to be hard-wired into us, as the neuroscientist Matthew Lieberman saw in his study of the brain, noting that the same 'neural machinery' is used in the experiencing of both physical pain and pleasure and social pain and pleasure.

A visit to Mother Teresa's tomb in Kolkata, seeing the testimony of her life, and where she spent her final days in the Missionaries of Charity compound, is a moving experience. In a city teeming with millions of people, walking the streets crowded with people from various castes, but particularly the Dalits, working in their menial jobs or begging, Teresa saw the pain of human disconnectedness.

> There is much suffering in the world—very much. And the material suffering is suffering from hunger, suffering from homelessness, from all kinds of disease, but I still think that the greatest suffering is being lonely, feeling unloved, just having no one. I have come to realize that it is being unwanted that is the worst disease that any human being can ever experience.[2]

---

[1] Archer, 2011, p. 20
[2] Teresa & Benenate, 2010, p. 14

While we may be aware of this in our own experience, and we may be familiar with the verses from 1 John above, obviously, not all human relationships are loving. We presume, or hope, that genuine love may be found, but utilitarian and contact-defined relationships are perhaps more common. Wittgenstein wrote of 'word games', not to trivialise language but to make the point that there are rules of the game when it comes to language and communication. In a similar way, there are 'relationship games' with rules that define-us-in-context.

One such relational rule in many languages concerns the second-person pronouns. Languages tend to differentiate between relationships that we may have with objects, even animals, and those with other human beings. The *It-You* distinction in English we understand well, and we use *You* to refer to other human selves. Martin Buber is famous for his writing concerning the *Ich-Du* (I-You) relationships. Buber's point is better expressed in older versions of English as I-Thou, as modern English does not make a distinction between You in a general sense and You as someone with whom we relate closely. When we read the 'King James English' or 'Shakespearean English' of the 17th century, we may think of the use of Thou (nominative singular), Thee (objective singular) and Ye (nominative plural) and their related verb forms as quaint but unnecessary today when You will suffice for all. Many languages, however, have maintained the distinctions, and they are very significant relationally. In English, "How are you?" will be appropriate in all relational contexts. In Spanish, however, to take just one language example, the pronoun used (formal, *usted* or familiar, *tu*) will depend on a range of things such as age, familiarity, social status, the particular setting, and local cultural preferences. Parents and children will use the familiar form, as will close friends. The formal form will be used when there is an age, class or social status difference, in a formal setting, or as a sign of respect. Friends may use the familiar *tu* in conversation before a formal meeting, but during the formal meeting, always use the formal *usted* with each other. Other languages, such as Japanese and Indonesian, have a variety of forms of the pronoun depending on relational circumstances. These grammatical constructions define, and are defined by, person-to-person relationships. In a Spanish context, an invitation to *tutear* is an invitation to another to use the familial *tu* with the inviter, meaning that they are happy to consider the other as being an equal in a friendly relationship.

Friendship

"Warren Buffett, . . . says his measure of success is, 'Do the people you care about love you back?' I think that is about as good a metric as you will find." (Bill Gates)[3]

---

[3] Gates, 2018, para. 7

The Bible uses a number of words that have been translated into English as "love". We may be familiar with C S. Lewis' work "The Four Loves" which commented on four of the terms from the New Testament: *eros*, *storge*, *philia*, and *agape*. These may be defined briefly as desire, or erotic attraction, familial love, friendship, and a deep, giving kind of love. Within the Church, we often find exhortations to engage in *agape* love, and 1 Corinthians 13 in particular is quoted. In that passage, the earlier English translations used the word 'charity' and that, linked with our modern understanding of charity, implies a giving love, a love that makes sacrifices for another. There are other terms found in the Scriptures that describe human relationships and bonding. It seems that the Bible does not include a term for the first flush of attraction, of romantic enchantment, we feel at the beginning of a relationship. It does, however, describe such feelings in some detail in the writings of Solomon, particularly in his Song of Songs. Another New Testament term is *xenia*, hospitality, or the love of the stranger— often used in the context of hospitality for which Eastern cultures are so well known, but perhaps it is often overlooked in individualistic Western cultures.

Within Christendom, however, a strong link is made between Jesus' sacrificial death and the need for us to love others in an *agape*, giving way. To this end, verses are quoted such as, "Greater love has no one than this, that he lay down his life for his friends" (John 15:13). While this may seem the ultimate ideal, and certainly is of importance regarding God's dealing with us, it may be seen as something of a starting point in a relationship. If a marriage is based solely on sacrifice for the benefit of the other, then the relationship will probably become unequal and one-sided—at least appearing to be one-sided to each if both are consciously sacrificing constantly for the other. It would seem that once the initial establishment of the relationship has been completed, or, on occasions, a sacrifice has been required—in an emergency, as it were—then the deeper mutuality of friendship needs to be sought. So, while sacrifice may be included in friendship, the emphasis is on simple reciprocity and mutuality. Jesus' sacrifice was a once-for-all beginning of relationship for us but a form of friendship was always intended to grow over time.

In a general sense, apart from pragmatic association of simply being with others and filial relationships, what we call 'friendship' appears to be one of the most common types of relationship to which we refer. Children in school have their 'besties' and trauma may result from broken relationships in the playground. Apart from the 'friends' we may have on social media, as adults, we tend to have fewer friends, but we would hope that the relationships are deeper and longer lasting. The comment has been made that one of Jesus' miracles was having 12 close friends when He was in his 30s! The notion of friendship has generated its own vocabulary in different cultures, including mates, buddies (buds), cobbers, companions, cronies, chums, sidekicks, and others. For us, the word 'friendship' has something of a 'warm fuzziness' about it, something with which we feel comfortable—for, fundamentally, friends are those with whom we feel comfortable and whole and a void is felt when a friendship is lost. Aristotle even went so far as to write, "For without friends, no one would choose to live." With references to earlier Greek philosophers, Aristotle noted that some believed that friendship was based on likeness, giving rise to expressions such as "birds of a feather flock together." Others, he noted, believed friendship to rely more on difference and complementarity, and the example he used was of different notes in music producing harmony. By whichever means friendship was produced, he saw it as being fundamentally beneficial:

> It helps the young, too, keep from error; it aids older people by ministering to their needs and supplementing the activities that are failing from weakness; those in the prime of life it stimulates to noble actions—'two going together'—for with friends, men are more able both to think and to act.[4]

It is interesting to see the logic of Aristotle's reasons for which friendships are sought: the good, the pleasant, and the useful. The good implies seeking a relationship that is good, or has some virtue, for us; the pleasant implies a relationship that will satisfy desires (such as a sexual relationship); and the useful implies a desire for a relationship that is purely utilitarian—it is useful for me or for my purposes. Aristotle noted that friendships based on utility and desire would usually be short-lived, but, of course, he did not have our advantage of God's revelation regarding the Fall of mankind into a sinful state, the consequences of which profoundly affect relationships. He did note, however, that "with respect to each there is a mutual and recognised love, and those who love each other wish well to each other in that respect in which they love one another."[5]

Augustine quoted Cicero's high regard for friendship: "Now friendship may be thus defined: a complete accord on all subjects human and divine, joined with mutual goodwill and affection."[6] Augustine, however, considered that true friendship "is not possible unless you bond together those who cleave to one another by the love which 'is poured into our hearts by the Holy Spirit who is given to us (Romans 5:5).'[7] Aristotle has been quoted also as saying, that friendship is, "one soul inhabiting two bodies" and this may bring to mind the indwelling of the Holy Spirit in the members of His Church—one Spirit inhabiting many bodies.

A distinction can be made between *agape* love and *philia* friendship. Voltaire drew on one distinction by saying that you could love someone but not particularly enjoy

---

[4] Aristotle & Brown, 2009, p. 142
[5] Ibid. p. 142
[6] Cicero & Shuckburgh, 2009, p. 15
[7] Augustine & Dods, 1871, p. 56

conversing with them if they are 'tiresome' or cannot be trusted with secrets. Friendship on the other hand, he described as a marriage of souls and such a marriage, he claimed, was only possible between 'virtuous' people.

An English Cistercian Abbot and writer of the 12th century, Aelred of Rievaulx, gave advice to a novice in his book, *Spiritual Friendship*. In it, he portrayed 'friendship' as the highest relational ideal. Writing this century, Marsha Dutton concurs with this high status definition of friendship—friendship that was seen in the mutual willingness of many Christian martyrs to sacrifice as "a thousand pairs of friends ready to die for each other."[8] Friendship, for Dutton, relates to Cicero's claim that from the Latin word *amor* comes *amicus* and from *amicus, amicitial*: from *love* comes *friend*, and from *friend*, comes *friendship*. Such a friendship is a covenantal one that is long-lasting (Proverbs 17:17). The book of Proverbs contains a number of other references to friendship, including the idea of a friend sticking closer than a brother (Proverbs 18:24).[9]

Statements such as these bring to mind other biblical references such as the verse quoted above: "No one has greater love than to lay down his life for his friends" (John 15:13). How powerfully significant then is Jesus claim to His disciples, "I have called you *friends*" (John 15:15)! To stand before the Creator and Redeemer who gave His life for us, and be known in a relationship of *friendship* is incomprehensible to us and yet that is a privilege He offers.

This also throws into perspective James 4:4, "You adulterous people, don't you know that friendship with the world is hatred toward God? Anyone who chooses to be a friend of the world becomes an enemy of God." God's concern here is not that we have an *eros* desire for the World, or even an *agape*, sacrificing love for it, but that we must not have a *philia*, reciprocal, mutual, covenantal bond with it.[10] This aligns with a warning from C. S. Lewis' *The Screwtape Letters*: "Prosperity knits a man to the World. He feels that he is 'finding his place in it', while really it is finding its place in him."[11]

Finally, there is another distinction that may be made between sacrificial, *agape*, love and friendship. The sacrifice or cost of *agape* love is something that is recognised or felt. Jesus went to the Cross, knowing what He was doing, conscious of the cost, and why. While sacrifice may be seen at times in friendship, for example, in the text above concerning laying down one's life for a friend, friendship has about it the idea of a habitual goodness extended to the other, regardless, or without thought of, any cost. Habitually, one may make a hot drink for one's spouse first thing in the morning—something done without thought of cost. It is simply a part of the plethora of things

---

8 Dutton, 2010, p. 60
9 See also Abraham and God (2 Chronicles 20:7); David and Jonathan (1 Samuel 20:42)
10 Other warnings include Deuteronomy 23:6 and Ezra 9:12.
11 Lewis, 2013, pp. 167–168

throughout the day that are embedded in a mutual and reciprocal friendship bound by a covenant. Are we able to reach a level of relationship with God, as Abraham apparently did, where we no longer 'count the cost' of our giving of time, finances, or ourselves? All of our lives in relationship with Him would then become simply something friends do. Given the inherent inequalities in our relationship with Almighty God, however, any idea of reciprocity becomes problematic. If, as an example, we take the 1855 words by Joseph Scriven that became the hymn, *What a Friend We Have in Jesus*, we see the one-sided nature of this friendship so often is seen to take:

> What a friend we have in Jesus
> All our sins and griefs to bear
> And what a privilege to carry
> Everything to God in prayer
>
> Oh, what peace we often forfeit
> Oh, what needless pain we bear
> All because we do not carry
> Everything to God in prayer
>
> Have we trials and temptations?
> Is there trouble anywhere?
> We should never be discouraged
> Take it to the Lord in prayer
>
> Can we find a friend so faithful
> Who will all our sorrows share?
> Jesus knows our every weakness
> Take it to the Lord in prayer

The cost of relating[12]

Apart from the sacrifice of *agape* love, other-centeredness (allocentrism) as opposed to egocentrism, as we have seen, involves the incursion of cost. The John 15:13 verse above illustrates the high cost that may be associated with relating closely. The costs considered here are those in relationships other than friendship. They may be seen, for example, in the preference parents give to their children, being willing to

---

[12] This section dealing with the cost of relationship is not concerned with costs as described in social exchange theories where the assessment of exchanges in relationships is in terms of cost-benefit analyses.

forego many things for the benefit of the child. These could include physical things, and in extreme cases, even food, as well as priorities of time allocation. In other relationships going the extra mile is not merely an add-on that may be considered but is seen as essential to the relationship.

At a different level, we see the cost of humans relating to God. In the Old Testament, this involved animal and other sacrifices and these were to be of the 'first fruits', animals without blemish, the finest and best. For the Hebrews, relating to their God was to be a costly business, and when they decided to discount their giving, and therefore their relationship, their God was not pleased (Leviticus 22:17–20). In the New Testament, we see the cost of Jesus' death in order to restore the relationship, and while this frees us personally from that cost, a cost was paid. A further cost for us is the price of discipleship, of obedience and dedicated allegiance. This usually involves the cost of being prohibited from doing all the things our sinful selves want to do. At the extreme, and recognising our desire to live, for so many, their allegiance has led to their torture and death. This is a very high cost indeed—though we must concede that it is insignificant when compared to the life to come.

Caring and giving of ourselves also involves a cost, perceived or real, of the partial loss of our identity. Further costs associated with relatedness are the cost of exposure, being vulnerable, or of losing something of the secret *me* that we guard so jealously. It also may involve the exposure of the me-life if we exhibit a degree of caring that may not be common in our society. As we do not exist in isolation, our self-concept is very much defined by a social definition of ourselves. This is because in order to really understand another in a relationship requires a change in our understanding of ourselves. Hans-Georg Gadamer wrote of us having a horizon of understanding that refers to the extent of our understanding from our viewpoint. In a relationship, a form of fusion of horizons takes place and, as well as seeing the other, we see ourselves differently, and this, as Charles Taylor and others have pointed out, comes at a cost to our identity. As Taylor explains, it alters our understanding of ourselves and creates an 'identity shift' in us. Karl Marx understood the personal identity cost in terms of a merging into social and political power, where the individual, in his philosophy, loses much of their individual being in order to become a 'species-being'. For many millions, of course, the outworking of Marxist theory by his disciples was to represent not only identity cost but the loss of freedom and life itself. His own ideas, by themselves, appear to be much more benign, but they still were founded on a costly change on the part of the individual.

Today, in the social media-drenched Western cultures in which we live, not merely identity cost is a problem, but identity theft is a real possibility. The accessibility of social media and the distancing from others via technology allows us to play with relationships in ways that had not been previously experienced. We may be aware of the potential risks involved, and much has been written about them, but perhaps involved in the potential for an identity cost, there is a certain, intriguing, risk-potential frisson that actually invites engagement.

Some historical contexts

We have been pondering human groupiness about as long as there have been humans to group. In the pre-industrial era, the family, tribe, and village defined relationships. With the industrial age came the need to bring unrelated people together to work, and in order to provide some level of cohesion to complete tasks. Apart from using brutal and dictatorial practices, industrialists, sociologists, and business leaders sought efficiencies and therefore felt the need to define and categorise human relationality. Given this context, there has been a tendency often to promote transactionalist considerations regarding power and economics between human beings.

Max Weber used the German terms *Gesellschaft* (society) and *Gemeinschaft* (community) to distinguish two ideal or pure states of human-to-human engagement within economic frameworks, but noted that they do not lie on a temporal continuum. In other words, Weber concluded that history has not shown a movement from *Gesellschaft* to *Gemeinschaft* but that both exist contemporaneously. More will be said about these German terms later, but we might note here that they had been defined and brought into the social sciences much earlier by Ferdinand Tonnies in 1887. Tonnies had concluded that when humans associate, we do so as organic life in community, or mechanistically in a society. While the two group structures may appear to be similar superficially, there are very distinct differences in the way the group members relate.

Educational institutions, as groupings of learners, whether as compulsory groupings such as schools, or non-compulsory, such as in higher education, function on a contractual basis: the selling and consuming of knowledge and skills as products, as it were. This may work against the idea of creating a community but it also reflects our culture. Sergiovanni saw the breakdown of the idea of community in schools as being in relation to the dissolution of community in culture at large, and claimed that schools have come to be seen as 'organisations' rather than communities. This is despite the human need for relationships. Purposeful school communities, he claimed, should be places where a sense of community of mind binds community members together as they share a common ideology and purpose, and not for other, utilitarian purposes.

Church congregations also may be seen as communities of learners, existing within the Body of Christ, His eternal Church. We might say, therefore, that fundamental to any discussion is the fact that as Christians we are not alone. Our tasks for His purposes are not carried out purely as individuals, nor even as groups. As Herman

Bavinck wrote of the whole of humanity bearing the image of God: "The image of God is much too rich for it to be fully realised in a single human being, however richly gifted that human being may be."[13] As His image bearers, we may also note that God is, as it were, the God of the verb *to be*. He declares Himself to be *I Am* in the Old Testament, and His eternal being is captured in the New Testament descriptions of Jesus as the Alpha and Omega—the Beginning and the End. As those created in His image, we have *being*. We are human *beings*. We do really exist, as Descartes concluded, unlike the techno-solipsistic characters in the film, *The Matrix*. Our relationships are set in this dimension of being-ness in space and time. We, as beings created by the *I Am*, relate to Him and other beings created by Him, and we, and our relationships, are set within the stream of His time.

The common enemy

Before leaving this chapter, we might briefly consider the issue of the common enemy. Politicians famously use this to develop or maintain cohesion within the electorate, and leaders of organisations, including those in Churches or educational institutions, may also be seen to use it. There is something in the collectivist part of our makeup (and more will be said on this later) that seeks a sense of belonging to the ingroup and repelling all others. This may be to promote cohesion, but it is also to give one a sense of safety in belonging, especially if the outsiders are proclaimed to be a clear and present danger to us. It is not uncommon, therefore, for varying degrees of a sense of outrage to be experienced and expressed with respect to claimed threats or calamities. This outrage seems to confirm for us our identity and our moral rectitude. It also provides a sense of safe inclusion in a particular cultural group and becomes a powerful motivator for what may otherwise be seen as irrational thinking and behaviour: "Outrage is a destructive drug that satiates our primal desire for group solidarity."[14]

The practical outworking of this takes various forms and may include joining forces with those previously considered enemies. We are familiar with the expression, "The enemy of my enemy is my friend." This combative aspect of human groups seems also to be linked to our human desire, starting with the Fall, to struggle against adversity. And if there isn't adversity or an adversary, then, as conspiracy theories show, we will invent them! Being quite comfortable with the idea of conflict, and strongly desiring the safety and security of belonging to a group of like-minded people, work together to promote so much of the harsh commentary on social media. Great care must be taken by us, however, in dealing with any resulting ideological wars. While it is proper to defend the truth, this is problematic when such defence becomes strident and aimed

---

[13] Bavinck, 2004, p. 577
[14] Harinam & Henderson, 2019, para. 58

at manipulation. Unfortunately, reactions such as these are seen all too frequently in churches, Christian schools and colleges, and Christian organisations, where leaders promote a strong them-and-us mentality in order to promote cohesion (i.e., to keep their kingdom together) or to promote loyalty to them.

3. Individuality

"Now more than ever the claim to focus everything on ourselves is illusory—to make individualism the guiding principle of society has proved to be illusory." (Pope Francis)[1]

"Due to excessive individualism and subjectivism and a lack of common good, the dominant modes of thinking and acting are destructive nihilism and immanent narcissism."[2]

Individualism plays a very significant role in all of our Western institutions and organisations, and it is referenced frequently, but perhaps we have not considered its nature or its setting within relational networks. We have come a long way in the development of individualism and Yuval Levin has even used the term 'hyper-individualism' to describe sections of 21st-century Western culture. What we observe around us as a generalised phenomenon is a range of taken-for-granted Western cultural traits focused on the individual. For us, in the West, this will often appear to be simply normal; it is right, it is the way things are, and we base many of our assumptions of reality on this perception. This is despite the fact that our initial self-understanding is one of family and group membership. At least in the West, therefore, it is only with time that we actually learn to be individuals. While for human beings, relationality is evident from birth, and possibly pre-birth, Enlightenment-sourced individualism and sociality are states into which we are enculturated. In cultures such as in the United States, where the Declaration of Independence contains the, perhaps utopian, phrase regarding "unalienable rights" of life, liberty and the pursuit of happiness, these "rights" become deeply embedded in the national culture and the individual psyche. We see constant reminders of this in the news, with "right to life", "black lives matter", and "all lives matter" movements, individuals claiming their right to freedom to do a wide range of things (bear arms, not wear face masks, etc.), and cries for justice (or vengeance) when one's happiness or contentment is threatened.

One might imagine a development in thinking from Descartes' 17th-century concern with solipsism (the Matrix-like idea that reality exists only in our minds) and that only

---

[1] Brockhaus, 2020
[2] Bahovec, 2015, p. 335

those things exist that we can directly experience,[3] to the 18th-century Enlightenment thinkers and the objectification of everything outside the self. Individualism seemed to really come to the fore during 19th-century Romanticism, with an emphasis on, or priority given to, a subjective interpretation of experience. This came, particularly, as a reaction to the constraining structures of the factory societism of the Industrial Revolution. Then there was the concern of Søren Kierkegaard in the late 19th century regarding the self, leading him to be considered by many to be the father of existentialism: the 'I' exists, is important, and all thinking about reality must begin there. Existential philosophy grew in scope and influence during the early 20th century, particularly in Europe, and still has its influence today.

The acceptance of individualism in the West is presuppositional; it is a part of our unconscious definition of what is normal; it is built into our worldview assumptions, by our culture. This is so much the case that it means that sometimes the secularist roots of individualism remain unrecognised as such by many Christians. Individualistic relating, that is so dominant in Western societies, places the self at the centre, is certainly not communal at its core, and is even antithetical to communality. It becomes up to the individual to strive for their own happiness and fulfilment, while maintaining their 'rights', and their role in society, or the community, may be seen in utilitarian terms as being to ensure that the individual's rights are preserved.

The social order we know as individualism does not mean that individuals are confined to live isolated lives in the hermit sense, of course, but the rights and needs of the individual are frequently considered to have primacy. In individualistic cultures, individuals are claimed to have free will and agency and therefore act as unencumbered selves without the necessity of an existential embeddedness within relational networks. At the same time, there may be a perceived moral obligation to promote equal rights for individuals within the society. Claims may be made that all individuals are equal, for

---

[3] Regarding the idea that things only exist if we can see them, the Catholic theologian Ronald Knox penned the following whimsical limericks:

God in the Quad
There was a young man who said "God
Must find it exceedingly odd
To think that the tree
Should continue to be
When there's no one about in the quad."

Reply:
"Dear Sir: Your astonishment's odd;
I am always about in the quad.
And that's why the tree
Will continue to be
Since observed by, Yours faithfully, God."

example. At the same time, each individual is expected to operate out of a degree of self-interest and to be self-reliant. Given the variations in gifts and abilities across a population, ultimately, this must generate inequalities and envy. Conflicts also arise when the efforts of one individual to achieve their goals inevitably interfere with, or restrict, those of another.

This is not to say that individualism is necessarily always selfish in all scenarios. Jüri and Anu[4] found instances where increases in individualism actually appeared to lead to increased altruistic volunteering. Other research found that individualists could more readily volunteer to work with 'others' than those with a collectivist outlook. Research by Beilmann and Realo[5] also linked this tendency of individuals to volunteer to perspectives on personal responsibility and a desire to increase one's social capital in their social setting, thereby also bringing indirect advantage to them.

Each individual, of course, has his or her own cognitive, affective and experiential existence that is distinct from all others. Through enculturation and experience within a cultural setting, the individual tends to trust the individual, truth and meaning become individually discerned or defined, and trust outside the self may be limited. Truth is, therefore, often relativised, and ownership of truth is claimed by the self. Coexisting, believing, and acting tend to be for the benefit of the self, and, as seen in the examples above, altruistic actions are still strongly grounded in the individual. The actions of many individuals in individualistic Western countries during the COVID pandemic have evidenced this.

History

We accept the obvious conclusion that we are all individuals, each with our own set of knowledge, beliefs, assumptions, values, and feelings, all of which are encased in physical bodies that are distinct from all other human bodies. What follows is not a history of individualism as such but some brief comments pertaining to some features of individualism. Humans have no doubt thought about what it means to be an individual in one form or another since the beginning of our existence, and modern sociology theorists and researchers have been exploring the phenomenon for more than a century.

The pre-eminence of the individual that has become the individualism of Western cultures has a considerable history: one that has shown development through changes in historical and social conditions. It appears, however, that the emphasis on selfhood as we know it is a relatively modern phenomenon. Dumont referred to modern

---

[4] Jüri & Anu, 2004
[5] Beilmann & Realo, 2012

individualism as "an exceptional phenomenon" with no real agreement as to its origins, but one which had become the cardinal value of our, at least Western, societies.

> For some scholars, especially in countries where nominalism is strong, it has always been everywhere; for others it originated with the Renaissance or with the rise of the bourgeoisie. Most commonly perhaps, and according to tradition, the roots of the idea are thought to lie in our classical as well as in our Judeo-Christian heritage, in various proportions.[6]

Another perspective on the development of individualism comes from the changes in fundamental beliefs promoted, as mentioned, by the Enlightenment thinkers. Charles Taylor speaks of a "great disembedding"—a move from seeing humans as being embedded in a group of some sort, that group being embedded in the cosmos, and God being over the cosmos. These relationships, as James Smith points out, have been broken through Enlightenment disenchantment, then by social contract theories, and subsequently, and consequently, the rise of individualism. Interestingly, Bahovec linked the modern rise in individualism and subjectivism with a decline in traditional church affiliation in Europe, where there has been a substantial rise in 'seeker-ship' for alternative 'spiritual' experiences. He noted that sociologists of the mid-20th century had written extensively on the phenomenon and the importance of the Enlightenment on its development and that some seemingly non-individualist constructions, such as Hobbes social contract idea, actually are founded on individualistic assumptions.

Indicative of the evolution of individualism, language study by Cohen over the period 1828 to 2003 found that in England and the United States, there was a significant diminution of the use of shame-related words and a stronger emphasis on guilt-related words. More will be said on this later, but this indicated to Cohen a move from more collectivist cultures to more individualistic cultures. There appear, however, to be many other factors involved in the rise of individualism. Triandis, for example, observed the tendency towards smaller families, particularly those with only one child, that may experience a high degree of independence, and away from large families where relational rules must be applied to avoid chaos. His conclusion was that, "As societies become more affluent (individualistic), they also reduce the size of the family, which increases the opportunity to raise children to be individualists."[7] This may be applied to strong economies such as that of the United States, but in their developmental history, not all individualisms are the same. Bahovec saw a distinction between the classical form of individualism in the United States, where the perspectives of the individual and the community were somewhat in balance, and some more recent versions that tend

---

[6] Dumont, 2004, pp. 23–24
[7] Triandis, 1989, p. 510

to be more utilitarian and where the autonomy[8] of the individual takes precedence over the community.

Given that the teaching of the Church includes so much relating to loving each other and the development of interpersonal bonds, it is perhaps surprising to see that the teaching of the Reformation has been credited as another promoter of the development of individualism. This flowed from an emphasis on an inward communion of the individual with God, the priesthood of all believers, and our autonomy with regard to a knowledge of God effected by His indwelling Holy Spirit. In this regard, relationship distinctions have been drawn between Protestant, Roman Catholic, and Jewish groups in research by Colzato, van Beest and van der Wildenberg. Their work examined whether participants focused on an important object (a more individualistic response) or on its context (a more communal response). Their research results provided evidence that a preference given to global or contextual features was significantly "reduced in Calvinism, a religion emphasising individual responsibility, and increased in Catholicism and Judaism, religions emphasising social solidarity."[9] They noted further that the observed effect in Calvinists may emerge from teaching regarding what was referred to by the Dutch theologian and politician, Abraham Kuyper, as Sphere Sovereignty. The notion of Sphere Sovereignty, set within a context of a discussion of Church-State responsibilities, emphasised the idea that each part (sphere) of life has its own authority and responsibilities. Colzato, van Beest and van der Wildenberg noted that the application (correctly or incorrectly) of this concept in the Netherlands produced a pillarization within the society and promoted the idea that each person should mind his or her own business. At an individual level, one's 'business' was between the person and God, and the Protestant belief in the ability of the individual to communicate directly with God without the necessary mediation of any congregational context was also seen to promote individualism. At the level of state outcomes, Colzato, van Beest and van der Wildenberg saw in the writing of numerous authors, the strong emphasis on individualism in the United States as facilitating the rise of capitalism as well as the political constitution (as seen in the Declaration of Independence).

Human relationality in recent times has a strong connection with the idea of personal fulfilment and a desire for self-actualisation rather than of the group by the group, or of the self or group, by God. Presumably, this has contributed to the rise in concerns regarding identity crises, which are increasingly seen as the norm for humans. The ancient Greek injunction 'to know oneself' has been around for millennia,

---

[8] The notion of an autonomous individualism may be traced to the origin of 'autonomy': *auto nomis*—a law unto oneself. We might then ask, do the Scriptures ever present us with a directive be independent from God and each other and to make our own laws for ourselves?
[9] Colzato, van Beest, van den Wildenberg, et al., 2010, p. 87

but the striving to meet our self-fulfilment needs seems to be a particular concern in our time. This, no doubt, flows from the thinking and writing of the late 19th century and early 20th century of authors such as Kierkegaard, Nietzsche, Sartre, Heidegger, and many others, concerning the meaning of the existence of the self. These were followed by transcendentalists who sought fulfilment in private experiences that were purported to lift one from the mundane conditions of everyday life in society, where one is seen to be at life's mercy. One feature of these two movements was the notion of alienation, of powerlessness, meaninglessness, and frustration, and it is little wonder that there has been a rise in self-fulfilment programs and the desire for self-actualisation in a context of alienation, God-is-deadness (Nietzsche), envy, and strong competition.

It may be difficult for us to see ourselves and the extent of our individualistic orientation in our culture clearly without referencing other cultures—seeing our own reflection as in a cultural mirror or contrasting ourselves with others. Dumont, comparing individualistic and holistic cultures, used an illustration from a section of religious society in India. In this case, within the context of a society's strict interdependence, individuals seeking ultimate truth may attempt to do so by foregoing social life in order to devote themselves to their own destiny by their own means. "When he looks back at the social world, he sees it from a distance, as something devoid of reality, and the discovery of self is for him coterminous, not with salvation in the Christian sense, but with liberation from the fetters of life as commonly experienced in the world."[10] Dumont describes the world renouncer, who may live a life of solitude or with a group of like-minded hermitic truth-seekers, as being "individuals-outside-the-world". Westerners, by contrast, tend to be individuals-in-the-world.

Some other features of individualism

When given agency and a self-locus for understanding life, human beings, endowed as we are with senses and appetites, have a tendency to seek comfort and pleasure— to eschew discomfort and pain in their various forms. Individuals living in close proximity will usually find that envy may lead to competition, even degenerating to a struggle that can be a no-holds-barred version of social Darwinism: of 'Devil take the hindmost'. The idea of self-containment, where social relationships are represented as entanglements that inevitably interfere with the pursuit of self-chosen goals, may lead to consideration of the particular costs that are involved with relating. There is the cost of having limited help available when needed, and there is the cost of obligation to others if help is proffered, and these may colour one's independent living and goal seeking.

This does not mean, however, that in any effort to help others, there are not behaviours that may well be aimed also towards some benefit for the individual. Such

---

[10] Dumont, 2004, p. 25

behaviours, as noted before, tend to be linked to self-fulfilment in one form or another, but the removal of an individual from a society also carries with it the costs for the society of the denial of any benefits the individual may bring to it. There are also costs to the individual through denial of sociation, the importance of which was discussed earlier, and the absence of support of others when needed. More profound than those costs is the removal of an important feature of self-concept development. Sociologists such as Charles Cooley and George Herbert Mead, early last century, saw that our self-concept evolves in the presence of social interactions. Much of the way we see ourselves is as reflected in the reactions of others to us, and this has been referred to as our "looking-glass-self", or as we see ourselves, as it were, in a social mirror.

This is an important consideration in the context of this book and its themes, where the depth of relatedness to others is seen at different levels in different cultural and practical contexts. This is despite the efforts by many to set out by themselves to "find themselves", or seeking to "know oneself", independent of others and the attendant relational and cultural constraints or interference. Any claim to a pure and noble form of individualism, however, is idealistic and ignores the influence of the Fall on humankind, not to mention human history. Many writers in the West in recent years, however, have shown a preoccupation with the idea of the individual's free will, or agency, as they try to understand our decision-making processes, but this is an outworking of the rejection of any idea of a God who may have control in some way.

Some Christian connections

A problem with radical individualism is that it tends to eliminate aspects of ethics or morality from our human existence. As Christians, we look to the Scriptures for God's guidance in terms of ethics and morality, and this includes visions of how we are to relate to others. Postlapsarian (after the Fall) humans in the West have a natural bias towards independence and natural individualism. Since the choice made in committing the first sin, we have tried to declare and practice this independence, despite the fact that we are never isolated as individuals, nor are we independent. God is always there, over and through His Creation. From Eden, relationship, or the potential for relationship, with Him is always present. Only in materialism (the belief that only the physical cosmos exists) is there even the possibility of an individual—a human—being devoid of essential and functional relationships. While a radical and non-relational individuality may arise only out of a denial of God's existence, the 'otherness' of God signifies that any relationship with Him must therefore be vastly different quantitatively and qualitatively from human relationships. Perhaps the thing that most blurs the relationship that human beings may need to have with God is the individualistic statement by God: *I Am*. Humans, following Satan's lead, seek divinity and covet the '*I am*' for ourselves.

Those who reject the very idea of there being a God, wanting to be their own 'I am', insist on their right to choose, and to choose to be unique. Backgrounded by relationship, however, the gift of individual agency, the ability to choose and act, was given first by God in the account in Genesis 1:28–30:

> God blessed them and said to them, "Be fruitful and increase in number; fill the earth and subdue it. Rule over the fish of the sea and the birds of the air and over every living creature that moves on the ground." Then God said, "I give you every seed-bearing plant on the face of the whole earth and every tree that has fruit with seed in it. They will be yours for food. And to all the beasts of the earth and all the birds of the air and all the creatures that move on the ground—everything that has the breath of life in it—I give every green plant for food." And it was so.

Scripture is replete with other examples of God's people acting on this agency and while God's attention has been directed at His 'people', Israel, and His Church, as corporate entities, the voices of individuals are heard constantly. To take just one example, in the English version of the Psalter, we find through the one hundred and fifty Psalms, well over two thousand uses of the first person singular pronouns: I, me, my, mine. The engagement of the psalmists was a personal and individual one with their God, though their words were often meant to be prayed or sung in a congregational setting.

The books of the Bible have been written by individual human authors and often include stories of individuals. So, as we read the accounts of individuals in the Bible, we may have the impression that the Bible promotes a form of individualism but this is not a true or complete picture of what was happening in the family of God. Unlike those in the Middle East in Bible times, we, in the West, usually desire to be unique; to be individually differentiated, and perhaps ever more so, from others. God still insists, however, that regardless of our desires, we are to love God and love our neighbour. . . even as we love ourselves (Matthew 22:34–40).

Of course, individuals do matter to God. In Jesus' teaching, we see in His parables of the lost sheep, the lost coin, and the lost son (Luke 15) that the individual is treasured by God. Indeed, there is repetition of the joy of an individual found: "I tell you there will be more rejoicing in heaven over one sinner who repents than over ninety-nine righteous persons who do not need to repent" (vs. 7) and "In the same way, I tell you there is rejoicing in the presence of the angels of God over one sinner who repents" (vs. 10). We are reminded also of Jesus' encounters with individuals such as Zacchaeus and Nicodemus, a rich young ruler, of the raising of Lazarus, and many more. Jesus was concerned with individuals. As well as the gathered nation of Israel, and the designation of 'His people', we do see in the Old Testament God dealing collectively with His people as well as relating to individuals: "Ezekiel and Jeremiah in particular call God's people to account even as they highlight the individual responsibility of each person (Ezek. 18; Jer. 31: 29– 30)."[11] In the New Testament, we see the members of His Church being described variously as branches of a vine, body parts, and stones in a building. In each case, while the emphasis is on the whole vine, body, and building, the argument being put is that these are constructed from individuals. There is incorporation, and very strong relationships exist between the individuals, but we are not given the impression of a homogenised 'lump' devoid of identifiable 'parts'.

Of course, there are instances of groups responding to God's calling, such as those we see illustrated in the story of Jonah regarding the turning of Nineveh, and presumably in the conversion of the Philippian jailor's family. In collectivist cultures, it can be common for significant decisions, such as turning one's allegiance to Jesus, to be made at the family level. Some years ago, while on the mission field in South America, a young friend brought a friend of his to our house, saying that she wanted to become a Christian. The Gospel was explained and her questions were answered. Finally, she was asked if this was a step that she wanted to take and she confirmed that it was . . . but she said she must go home and talk it over with her family. It was a family decision and not an individual one. While this may seem strange to us in the individualistic West, other cultures may see this as being normal and would wonder why we would think we could make such a decision without consulting the family or tribe. It should be stated, however, that the New Testament contains a number of references to those who would follow Christ, where the relationship they have with family or culture was to be put to one side if it did not cohere with the relationship with Christ.

As mentioned, Martin Buber stressed the importance of the idea of an *I-thou* relationship between people and particularly between people and God. He commented that we engage with two different things: the idea of community, and the inability of modern humans to relate to each other. Escape from this difficulty, he said, is an achievement of the power of God that works in our relationship with Him. This relationship not only flows from God but is initiated by Him. While Calvinist theology has been blamed in some circles for the rise in individualism, it also contains the strong notion of covenant community and following in the footsteps of John Calvin, Abraham Kuyper wrote of the importance of the salvation of the individual with others.

> This is the testimony that, on the authority of God's Word, sealed by our personal experience, we shout aloud for all to hear: *grace is particular*. Nevertheless, that same child of God is something other than an isolated individual limited to himself. This individual is also part of a *community,*

---

[11] Stackhouse, 2018, p. 112

member of a *body*, participant in a *group identity*, enclosed within an *organism*. The *doctrine of the covenant* emphasizes and does justice to this truth . . . . Therefore, in Holy Scripture this sovereign, personal election never appears in any other manner but within the context of *covenant grace*. The *individual*, this *single soul*, must experience being incorporated into the *community* of the saints. We are elected personally, but together we are branches of the one Vine, members of the same body. For that reason, the confession of particular, personal grace is untrue and unscriptural unless it arises within the context of the *covenant*.[12]

Creating individualism

Finally, if we wished to create individualism, or even to try to facilitate the further development of an individualistic culture, there are several proven ways by which this may be accomplished. First, there is the proclamation of unrestrained and guilt-free desire. You can be whatever you want to be. Each person for themselves. If it feels good, then just do it. You can have whatever you want. Aim high. You can be whatever you want to be. These, and many similar sentiments relating to hedonism, promises of fulfilment, and the primacy of personal experience, can bombard a population of collectivists or communalists and, in time, will break down relational structures. They work particularly well because they feed straight into our fallen natures and ignite our desire to have, to possess, and to be gods. The second way is through indoctrination, or education. Long-term education, where an individualistic curriculum, as taught by devout individualists, will prove transformational. In this form of education, knowledge is deemed to be owned by the individual and is assessed individually. Truth becomes what the individual declares it to be. Knowledge that is gained is said to bring personal freedom to choose, something that resonates with the Genesis 3 account of the temptation.

These methods have been used with striking success in many cultures that traditionally have been collectivist or communal. This has been so much the case that in many of those cultures Western individualism is seen now as being either the norm or something to be actively sought—regardless of the benefits of the traditional ways.

Individualism, however, requires individual-specific resources. We can walk into a very large store in another country and know that we do not know anyone in the store, we do not have any sort of relationship with anyone, but we need resources—I need them for me. The stronger the individualistic isolation from others, the stronger the perceived personal desire to meet personal needs without reliance on others. The isolation of individualism, however, has its costs and as individualism has increased in

---

[12] Kuyper, Ballor, Grabill, Kloosterman, Van & Mouw, 2016, pp. 2–3.

our cultures, not unexpectedly, loneliness has become a very significant factor. (Research by the Angus Reid Institute in Canada in 2019 found that 23% of Canadians described themselves as being 'desolate' while another 10% described themselves as being 'lonely but not isolated'. Only 22% described themselves as being 'cherished'.) This has led to the proliferation of counselling and help groups, mindfulness programs, and even the development of government departments. (In the Church, one may wonder if this is part of the reason why so many Christian songs have been written in recent years that view Jesus as some sort of a 'buddy' or 'boyfriend'.) The deep relationship we are encouraged to have with our inner selves is usually presented in such a way as to provide an alternative to a deep relationship with God. If we are to have a relationship with a god other than ourselves, then the World encourages us to invent our own and to treat that god as some type of genie who is available to grant us wishes for our personal satisfaction. A Gospel of prosperity for the individual grows readily in such an environment.

4. Society

Churches, Christian schools, and other organizations, often seek to work together as communities, but typically function as societies.

A considerable amount of the time taken in our engagement with others is within the structured relationships of what we term here, societies. For most people, these societies include our employment as we relate to others in the workplace, to educational institutions, churches, and other organisations. We might note here that the congregating of human beings is not always a positive thing, and certainly, there can be societies whose purpose is evil. In the biblical account of the Tower of Babel, in Genesis 11, we see God dispersing humans who had wanted to congregate for the wrong purposes. We do speak, however, of 'Christian societies' and sometimes by this we mean societies whose intentions are honourable, or perhaps we might take T. S. Eliot's definition: "a society in which no one is penalised for the *formal profession* of Christianity."[1]

The feature of societies on which we are focusing here is their use of structured relationships. There usually will be strict or loose hierarchies and rules, either formal or informal, governing the way individuals relate to those above, below, or beside. We promote these structures in order to accomplish particular goals, and from experience, we know that there will be those who conform and those who may rebel. This is very familiar to all of us and is a particular point of concern for those in leadership positions. The relationship structures of businesses, factories, and organisations in general have been very thoroughly studied, and so this section is somewhat shorter than the other sections in the book, but some comparisons and biblical perspectives may be useful.

The interrelatedness of individuals required for achieving more than an individual may achieve, either in a summing of individuals or through synergy, usually requires structure, and we refer to that structure here as society. Most organised groups of individuals, therefore, will function at least to some extent as a 'society'. The path from individualism to society is not straightforward, given the West's preoccupation with the individual. In relational terms, given our felt need for relating to other human beings, even while inhabiting 'business' or 'factory' models, there is still a need for what Yuval

---

[1] Eliot, 1940, p. 5

Levin referred to as *mediating institutions*. These include the family, church, unions, and so on.

Structured societies, that have such a significant role in terms of shaping our desires, habits, attitudes, character, and so on, may be constantly constrained to respond and react rather than act, as they may be confronted frequently with the self-centeredness of radical individualists. Concerned with this, the literature pertaining to organised society structures covers things such as organisational leadership and organisational culture. This has been driven particularly by strong movements in politics, industry, and economics. The study of relationships in society has been focused particularly on these movements and is seen in many arenas, including the Marxian idea that a society is comprised of relationships, not individuals. Some scholars see social relationship study as being a theoretical pursuit, others as referring to practical methodologies, and still others see it as the foundation for studying all of life.

Societ-ism is sometimes seen as an ideology or foundation to a belief system, and as such has been considered to be an antonym for individualism. In general terms, societism, while not ignoring individuals, emphasises the well-being of a structured group as a whole and more particularly the purpose of the group. The structuring will usually be aimed towards a specific end and will usually include cohesion through leadership hierarchies, vision and mission purpose statements, constitutions, rules or laws, and controlling ideologies. As we see around us, societies may be from quite small to a mega-corporate level, or even at a national level. Notwithstanding the utilitarian and affective calling on humans to relate to each other, in practice, particularly in Western cultures, societal groupings do not extinguish individualism. In totalitarian societies, the individual may become forcibly absorbed to some extent into a society and forced to strive for the society's benefit, but in the West, or where the choice to belong is given, the self-interest of individuals will also be evident.

The word, society, comes from the Latin *societas,* which signifies individuals united for a common purpose. While we may reject societism as a primary foundational belief system to underpin our practice, it is obvious that all of our institutions function in some ways as societies: with individuals relating to each other in ways that will promote the achievement of specific, pre-determined organisational goals. Christian education institutions may function with quite strong societal features, churches somewhat less so, and other Christian organisations somewhere in between. Within each of these groups, however, there may develop sub-groups, with deep interactions or relationships other than those necessary in order to complete the task or reach the goals of the society. These within-society groups may have a strong sense of identity and engender a strong sense of belonging.

Societies tend to provide a certain mechanistic embodiment of group members, each member being a cog, as it were, in the machine. Individuals, left to themselves, may work independently to accomplish all manner of personal goals but in societal structures, individuals are brought together in order to serve larger purposes using multi-person functionality, and much or our culture is served by these. The need, or perceived need, for such structures has also seen the need for, and the extensive study of, leadership practices in order to coordinate groups toward outcomes. [More will be said with regard to biblical understandings of 'leadership' in relational frameworks in the final chapter of this book.]

The degree of trust between individuals in a society is limited to perceived utility, though trust may be ascribed to the societal structure in general, as well as to the leadership with responsibility for maintaining the society. Meaning in a society is defined historically or by leadership and maintained formally for the utilitarian purposes of society members and/or the leadership. Leadership and management are highlighted in societies as there is a need to coordinate, encourage, guide, cajole, reward, or perhaps even force society members to move in the direction of the society's goals and maintain some semblance of peaceful coexistence and coordination. The call, therefore, is for the collected individuals in the society to conform in order to act as much as possible as a single unit. As Stackhouse explains, however, tight conformity is not without certain dangers:

> Every society must insist on a certain amount of conformity of belief and activity, or nothing can be done together. But beyond what is necessary, our families and churches—like most groups—tend toward maximal conformity instead of maximal creativity. Cultivation of diversity can seem inefficient; it is, at least initially, more costly than uniformity in time, effort, and attention. But if we fail to provide places for different people to grow, and to grow together, we will alienate both our own "non-standard" brothers and sisters and also, in the case of churches and other Christian organizations, all those outside our company who might have wanted to join but now see that they would not be welcome as themselves. Such an attitude fosters a kind of social inbreeding that inevitably results in pathology. God has so arranged the world that we actually need a certain amount of diversity just to avoid going wrong, let alone to help us go more and more right.[2]

That said, the need to study societal structures, and their political implications as well as the rights of individuals, was noted in the 17th and 18th centuries by philosophers such as Grotius, Hobbes, Locke, Rousseau, and Kant. The idea of a social contract has already been mentioned. This posited the agreement to be

---

[2] Stackhouse, 2018, p. 235

incorporated into a society as transactional whereby a deal is struck between the leadership or governance of the society and the members. Such 'contracts', or "treaties and peace pacts", as Tönnies[3] put it, are to spell out the rights and responsibilities of both parties.

The establishment and maintenance of non-voluntary societies, such as the political societies into which we are born, requires strong governance. As with all other human endeavours, governance, leadership, and management are corruptible and may not serve the governed well . . . as exemplified in world news reporting almost on a nightly basis. At the same time, societal structures do provide the possibility of a framework for peaceful co-existence and social order, something Rousseau claimed was a "sacred right" of human beings,[4] though we know that some form of social contract is necessary in order for a society to function purposefully and peacefully. The idea of contractual rights and responsibilities predates Hobbes, Rousseau, et al., of course, and we see examples in Old Testament history where God, the founder and leader of Hebrew society, outlined His covenantal 'bill of rights' in Leviticus and Deuteronomy in particular.

Of course, given our fallenness, structures such as societies are complex and evidence our fallenness in both sides of the contract: the massed individuals, and the leadership or political governance. The Reformed theologian and philosopher, Herman Bavinck, in his work *The Christian Family*, wrote of the problems of the homogeneity of the "masses" of society:

> The history of the last half century has brought to light so clearly that nothing is as dangerous as generalizing and lumping everything together. There is not a single law that governs the entire development of society; there is not simply one theory that fits all the facts of reality; all events do not move along a single straight line. Just as in previous centuries, society exhibits the richest diversity; that diversity itself has increased to a large extent through the progress of science and technology, of agricultural industry, of trade and traffic. It is not the case that two classes stand in opposition against each other—the rich and the poor, entrepreneurs and employees, the rulers and the oppressed. Instead, life is infinitely varied. In every enterprise, there are large and small, strong and weak, between whom again there exists not a gap but differences of degree . . . . Modern society is no different in principle from previous ones and will not differ radically from the society of the future.[5]

---

[3] Tönnies & Loomis, 1957
[4] Rousseau & Cole, 1762–2016
[5] Bavinck & Kloosterman, 2012, p. 131

Gesellschaft

As we have seen, we cannot conclude that the formation and function of groups of human beings as societies is totally negative. Sociologists and educators such as Tönnies and Sergiovanni, however, may see a desired progression from *Gesellschaft* (society) to *Gemeinschaft* (community). This movement, and the prioritising of *Gemeinschaft* may seem desirable at an affective level, but in practice, there is a need for pragmatic, functional, societal structures for specific purposes. Institutions and organisations within our Western cultures cannot operate without a functional society framework where individuals work together, perhaps without ever forming deep relationships, in order to achieve specific goals. Of course, we would want them to relate more deeply, and that is certainly biblical, but some forms of societal structures are still required for corporate goal achievement. Inhabited by fallen human beings, a school, a factory, or perhaps a very large church, may exist to serve a range of purposes without deep relationships. Without the structures of a society, however, people in a deeply related group may struggle to achieve their own sub-goals. Both *Gesellschaft* and *Gemeinschaft* forms, therefore, appear useful in their own way. We might, however, take note of a thought-provoking warning from Glenn Tinder regarding what we might term exclusive or extreme societism:

> The political meaning of Christianity, then, does not lie in the ideal of a Christian society for no such society can exist . . . . Society is the unity of human beings in subjection to one another and to the worldly necessities underlying custom, law, and governance. The terms Christian and society cannot logically be joined.[6]

This is an interesting statement, but it is one that relies on a particular meaning of 'society'—one that includes subjugation. All too often, fallen human beings seek control of the structures of a society for personal power or greed fulfilment purposes. Unfortunately, this has been seen all too often within even Christian institutions.

In conclusion, the uncomfortable truth for our churches and Christian organisations is that while the idea of *community* is emphasised and lauded, the reality is that at a leadership or governance level, most seek *society* as the highest priority. Leaders of groups of Christians may encourage deeper inter-personal relationships between group members, but, fundamentally, it is the structure of the group—the rules, the constitutions, the hierarchies, compliance, and adherence to the vision and mission— that is seen to be necessary in order to maintain the group's existence and achieve its goals. Without those things, the fear is that the group will either not adhere to the 'required' vision and mission, create an alternative vision and mission, splinter, or dissolve. It, therefore, may be true in some cases that an ardent plea for the formation

---

[6] Tinder, 1989, p. 61

of deeper *community* relationships could be an attempt to pull a group back to the purposes of a particular *society*.

5. Community

The proactive building of community will always be an elusive ideal because we try to squeeze it into the structures of a society.

"Everyone says they want community and deep friendship. However, because it takes accountability and commitment we run away"[1]

T he title of this book points to the formation and maintenance of community in Christian organisations, institutions, and other groupings of human beings. As mentioned, this is something toward which Christians strive and yet we seem to fall short often, for reasons such as those mentioned in the previous chapter. We recognise, however, that there are elements of *koinonia*, of fellowship, sharing in common, of 'community', or communitarian features, within all human groups, particularly Christian ones. Perhaps the difficulty arises because we hold to a definition of community that is difficult or impossible for fallen human beings to fulfil. As Christians, the expectation is that we will 'get along with' other 'brothers and sisters' as commanded in Scripture. Of course, the injunction of Jesus to love each other (John 13:34) demands a much deeper commitment than merely getting along together, so a desire for community, in a sense, is setting the bar quite low. Our hope, however, is that it may therefore be obtainable. In this chapter, we will look at some different perspectives on community—how it is seen and how a communitarian framework may lie as a category in the notional relationship series.

The idea of community may often be conflated with what Kaplan referred to as a "sense of community," or the feeling we have that comes from the positive experiences of friendship or close relationships with others in a group. We might first note in passing, therefore, that while for most of us the word community has some emotional attachment, the word has multiple meanings and is not always seen in a positive light. The term may be confusing, and one on which there is no strict, universal agreement. At times, it becomes weaponised, as it were, to be used as an emotionally powerful term that may be used by a speaker or writer to advocate a particular point. It has a "Mom and apple pie" type of ring to it, against which one may be disinclined to argue. Many academics, therefore, find the term of little use in terms of rigorous theory

---

[1] Keller, 2019

development. If we put aside this perspective and any negative academic dispositions, in general terms, we know the word community as a descriptor of relationship and more than simply what we might mean by a 'group'.

Considering a political perspective, Mojmir Križan was concerned with the unsettled nature of national-level societies in the post-communist era, as the cohesion of forced communalism was removed and he concluded that the best way to reduce fear, apathy, or unhealthy nationalism was to promote the idea of community, and he named this approach communitarianism. Križan further stated that: "Belonging to a community is a *sine qua non* [an essential] of the very morality and dignity of man, modern liberal democratic societies have to be understood as communities of communities."[2]

As Christians, we may consciously or unconsciously tend to think in terms of moving from one relationship framework to another, presumably one that is in some way better. In the West, we therefore may think it worthwhile to move away from individualism and societism, towards a fraternity founded on a loving relationship. We may think of loving in interpersonal relationships as acting in a loving manner, in terms of *doing* things pertaining to the relationship, but the essence is to be '*being* in relationship', and this is usually based on a degree of things held in common or, to use the term often used in intimate relationships, compatibility.

> Community as a term depends upon its root, which equally exists in common, commune, communication. Community then implies a sense of holding something in common, sharing and communing with one another. It is in this sense that we hold as basis for understanding community today. Not a thing created out of people happening to share a location or interest, but a set of processes and practices, actions that are constantly moving and changing, continually creating and transforming the communal. The term we use is 'common being-ness', the action of being in common. It is this which shows us the centrality of inter-relationality for understanding the actions and processes of community.[3]

This seems to have become more difficult in our current age. Zygmunt Bauman claimed that in our post-modern world, the only certainty is change, and he therefore rejected the term post-modern, replacing it with the term 'liquid modernity'.[4] The liquid modernity nature of our human environment limits relationships, necessarily rendering them short-lived, shallow, or non-existent. The idea, or ideal, of having-in-common, therefore flexes and shudders as individuals, circumstances, and relationality morph with constant changes. At the same time, as people share a community spirit and

---

[2] Križan, 1997, p. 152
[3] Studdert & Walkerdine, 2016, p. xii
[4] Bauman, 2018

purposes change, the community will change. If all or most community members are happy with the change, then the community, rather than splintering, may persist and strengthen.

Individualism may imply a non-, or limited relationality, and societism implies structured relationships, but communitarianism implies volition. In most countries, we are free to associate voluntarily. This implies an act of the will on the part of community members. "To the extent that communal obligations exist, they can be justified only insofar as they conform to the voluntary principle. Communities, with all of their supposed differences, must be recast as mere voluntary associations."[5] This has implications for Christian organisations. Teachers and parents may join a Christian school voluntarily, but in general, the students do not. What implications might this have for developing a school community? Churches, generally, are joined voluntarily, and perhaps this implies an easier transition to community, but what of those who, for various reasons, feel that they must attend (for example, the children of attendees)? What implications might this have? Employees in Christian organisations may join for economic reasons. How might this affect the sense of community? In higher education institutions, a range of factors will be at play, including adherence to campus rules, compliance with state-set requirements, teaching structures, and so on. Additionally, on-campus living, off-campus living, and online learning all have significant implications. The difficulty, in the West at least, is that there are always individualism and society-forming pressures with which we must contend. The community type of relationships, however, are sought in order to serve to fulfil specific relational needs that we cannot fulfil in individualistic isolation. We may even link this with our health, as Wendel Berry did when he described the idea of community in its fullest sense as being "the smallest unit of health and that to speak of the health of an isolated individual is a contradiction in terms."[6]

With the coming of the industrial age and the move from agrarian cultures to industrialism, Tönnies saw a resulting shift from *Gemeinschaft* (or "sacred" community) to *Gesellschaft* (or "secular" society). Tönnies provided a very useful distinction between the ideas of community and society: in a community, we remain united despite forces that would separate us, whereas in a society, we remain separated as individuals despite the efforts made to unite us.

The commonalities that tie us together as humans are varied. Daniel Bell saw the foundations of community relationship lying in what he termed three dimensions. First, there are the commonly identified "communities of place" where a group of individuals inhabit a common geographical location. Second, there are "communities of memory"

---

[5] Koyzis, 2017, para. 9
[6] Berry, 1994, p. 2

where members of a group share a history that is morally significant and therefore members usually share common interests. Finally, there are "psychological communities" where face-to-face interactions are the norm, and there is a degree of altruism expressed in trust and co-operation. Apart from their societal aspects, schools, churches, colleges, and businesses provide geographical, historical, and psychological contexts where meaningful inter-human relationships may flourish. Individuals become bound to others by developing a community mindset and some level of shared ideology or belief system. We might note here that the connectedness we may feel in congregational meetings, or in educational settings, is usually not too difficult to achieve, and it can be enough to engender significant meaning-making in common. For Christians, as members of the Body of Christ (Romans 5:30), as living stones built into His spiritual building (1 Peter 2:5), the growth of this communion, quantitatively and qualitatively, is to be our main task after worship. We can have friends who are non-Christians, but we cannot have a deep relationship with them as we do not share the same fundamentals (see 2 Corinthians 6:17).

While not having the depth of communal relationships, the 'we-ness' of community means that a degree of allocentrism [other-centredness], as opposed to egocentrism, must apply to at least some degree for an individual to join a community. The interactions between community members signify some level of influence in each direction. This implies a potential for change and therefore an identity cost to the individual—a cost that must be balanced against the perceived benefits or rewards of joining the community. Anne Snyder has made the comment that: "In a North American context increasingly allergic to constraints imposed from beyond the self, there are fewer and fewer examples of the rich kinds of community we crave—few want to compromise their privacy and surrender their freedom."[7] The benefits, however, include meeting the need to relate, feeling included, wanted or needed, and achieving greater purposes. Studdert and Walkerdine's term "communal being-ness" was used to describe the organic nature of "being in common".[8] The benefits that accrue from interconnectedness, shared understandings, norms and values, and so on, is referred to as "social capital". Social capital applies to the resources and benefits to which one has access through inhabiting a purposeful network of other human beings[9], and where each member has access to the social capital of the group as a whole. While this social capital may not be traded, as dollar

---

[7] Snyder, 2020, para. 3
[8] Studdert & Walkerdine, 2016
[9] We should note that while recognising the importance, particularly in the business world, of such concepts as networking, cooperation, collaboration, and partnerships, these are not a focus of this work.

capital may be, it certainly can be modified or even manipulated through the community relationships and the relative contributions of each member.

Large aggregations of human beings are very complex and dynamic systems that cannot simply be explained, defined, or reduced with reference to the individual components. The sociologist, Sawyer, used systems theory to explain what he and others have termed 'emergence' to define the materialisation of relationship structures within groups. While Sawyer and other sociologists have drawn mechanistic systems theory parallels with computers, which are much less complex than human beings, they do have a point. There is something in their argument regarding groups of human beings being synergistic, where the whole is greater than the sum of the parts.

As we have seen, most groups, including Christian ones, tend to function as societies and usually include some form of contractual transaction. For educational institutions, it could be seen in the payment of fees for a service provided, in businesses, work is exchanged for wages, and so on. In churches, different *quid pro quo* transactions also take place. The congregation members may see the exchange in terms of perceived quality of the worship music or the teaching, or other services offered, in exchange for their attendance or financial contributions. While inter-member relationships could be community-oriented, perhaps the subconscious contracts that are made with the church as a whole may be society-based.

It may be argued that the dissolution of a sense of community in our cultures in general has also interfered with the development of community within such entities as churches and educational institutions. This leads them to be perceived in the population as organisations rather than communities. That said, it is very common for them to have within them, or across different ones, communities—most commonly, 'communities of practice'. So, as well as having a being-ness together, members of communities may also act together. Wenger describes communities of practice as being comprised of individuals, "bound by what they do together—from participating in lunch-time discussions to solving difficult problems—and by what they have learned through their mutual engagement in these activities."[10]

There is an automatic relationship response to forming such groups in order to meet the primal, human need to relate. We recognise that to achieve quality relationships, there is also a need for the fundamentals of community groups: *commitment*. For a community to exist and function, community members must be committed to the existence of the community, even though any vision or mission may not be well defined or understood, and they must be committed to each other. It is that bonding in particular that defines community. It is the establishment of a '*we*' from a diverse collection of '*Is*'.

---

[10] Wenger, 2018, para. 7

This bonding requires not a contract but a covenant. As Križan expressed it, "*humans need each other*, they prosper best in close relationships and stable, solidary associations. Only in such associations—based upon a *covenant*, a moral bond of love and identity, and not on *contract*—can they develop their capabilities and conduct a satisfactory life."[11] This, of course, is the type of relationship God sought to have (Old Covenant) and seeks to have (New Covenant) with His people. Under a covenant relationship with God and with fellow community members, geographical space is shared as God brings people together, meaning is shared through His Word and the inspiration of the Holy Spirit, God's values are shared, and God's purposes (vision and mission) for humanity are shared.

A brief look at other cultural settings

Communitarian interrelationships would seem to exist in all cultures, as one might expect if it is a consequence of our being made in the image of a relational God. Originating in Indonesia, for example, the phrase *gotong royong*, which may be translated into English as "cooperation in a community" or "communal helping of one another", is used to express communal cooperation. Describing the Indonesian cultural context, the anthropologist Clifford Geertz also included the terms *rukun* ("mutual adjustment"), *gotong royong* ("joint bearing of burdens"), and *tolong-menolong* ("reciprocal assistance") to describe the governance of social interactions.[12] Language and cultural relationship practices are inextricably entwined, and many cultures use terms to indicate important forms of communal cooperation within the culture. (For example: Cherokee Indians (*gadugi*), Finns (*talkoot*), Philippinos (*bayanihan*), Kenyans (*harambee*), Turks (*imece*), Jewish/Russian (*subbotnik*), Norwegians (*dugnad*) and Irish (*meitheal*).) In earlier times in the UK and in the USA, notably in Amish communities, working together for a 'barn raising' was common. Amongst the indigenous Quechua people of the South American Andes, the terms *minka* or *ayne* are used to refer to favours given, such as the sharing of labour and tools at sowing or harvest times. Harmonious relationships are essential, obviously, for a close-knit communitarian existence, and working with others and eating together during community projects no doubt promotes bonding.

It is important to recognise, however, that these activities, such as *ayne*, involve considerable trust between community members. With *ayne*, the trust is that the work 'donated' will be repaid in kind. In the application of *pasanacu* where money is lent between Bolivian village members without documentation—there is simply the word of the borrower that it will be repaid at some stage. This adds a different flavour to the

---

[11] Križan 1997, p. 156
[12] Geertz, 1983

notion of cooperation in a community, and we can see that over time, perhaps centuries, and with changing economies and technologies, expressions of community may devolve into something more akin to those in a society. The *ayne* help given at harvest time may not be out of the goodness of one's heart, though it could be, but is based also on obligation: given with the expectation that when it is your harvest time, the others will come to help you.

The work of a group towards a specific purpose for the group usually will require some form of leadership, and therefore, the pure sense of community breaks down. In the Bolivian example, projects such as building roads, drainage systems, sports fields and so on obviously require coordination and leadership in some form. In these cases, where there is no possibility of being paid back, the obligation is usually enforced by the village leadership with a system of fines. If this conscription practice grows, the community may be expected to break down into a society or an organisation.

Knowledge

Human beings not only relate to each other, but we also communicate with each other. We share knowledge. We may be able to invent our own 'private language', but we can only use spoken or written language as a communication medium if meaning has been developed and agreed upon with others. Our faith, in the general sense, is intimately connected to language. Its principles are transmitted by language, and the meaning of the language is developed in the community. The creation and maintenance of meaning through sharing is foundational to social and communal relationships. Individualism has promoted learning theories of radical and not-so-radical constructivism, where the individual is encouraged to discover knowledge and meaning for themselves. The social constructivist theories of Lev Vygotsky and others have focused on meaning construction in relationship, and we recognise that truth and knowledge are defined by sharing in community.[13] We learn the basic meaning of a word or phrase perhaps as children, and as we grow and use language to interact with others, our understanding of the meaning of the word or phrase evolves and is refined. Our understanding of truth, or what makes something true as far as we can see, depends to a great extent on the interpersonal relationship contexts for that truth. As well as in education, this is an important consideration for Christians as we share the truths of the faith with our children and with others, developing relationships and using familiar linguistic rules and a vocabulary with a shared meaning.

---

[13] The seventeenth century mathematician, Blaise Pascale, had noted the construction of meaning in communities of practice and his advice to a friend who claimed to be almost a believer, was that he should join a church community. Through engagement in the practices of the Christians in community, Pascale felt that his friend would come to a point of acceptance of the Gospel.

We might note that modern technology and so-called 'social' media have added another layer of complexity to relationality and meaning construction. With the advent of Internet communications, new language structures and meanings have developed and continue to transform and evolve. In her studies of social media posts, Grechen McCullock has discovered that the meanings of words, sentence structures, and even the acronyms invented within the media subtly change through their use as social media community members adapt to the medium and seek to express themselves. She noted, for example, that while a full stop in written English is a useful and necessary punctuation item, in text messages, it is taken as an abrupt ending. (For example, "I have it" compared with "I have it.") The now familiar lol began with the simple meaning of the original words, laugh out loud. Current users, however, tend to use it to soften a comment, to indicate irony, or as an expression of passive aggression. The intended and received meaning of the communication becomes very heavily dependent on the relationship that exists between sender and recipient, and these relationships are set within meaning-creating cultures and subcultures. This is particularly important for Christians speaking with those outside their meaning-making community. Obviously, we would avoid using terms such as justification or propitiation, which for non-Christians would be meaningless, certainly in the senses we would mean. But, in our Bible-ignorant cultures now, such terms as sin, love, forgiveness, or even Jesus and God will not have the meanings for others that they have for us.

To take another example, many know that Australians will often insult each other, not because they are enemies but as an expression of friendship. It appears that the deeper the insult, the stronger the friendship. In effect, what is transpiring is that one person (usually male!) will be intending to communicate with their insult something like, our relationship is so strong that it can withstand this insult. It may therefore be seen as a type of bonding joke. [It should be noted that if the insult and relationship bond do not match exactly, the insult becomes just an insult, so being able to distinguish accurately is a skill best left to the experts!]

In Christian circles

> *"For the blessedness of a community and of an individual flow from the same source; for a community is nothing else than a harmonious collection of individuals."[14]*

The Scriptures contain many references to living in community and the attitudes, values, and actions that should be evident in community members. As an example, in 1 Peter 3: 8 & 9 we read: "Finally, all of you, live in harmony with one another; be

---

[14] Augustine, 1871, p. 24

sympathetic, love as brothers, be compassionate and humble. Do not repay evil with evil or insult with insult, but with blessing". In this regard, Jobes highlights the Greek words for 'brotherly love' (*philadelphos*) and 'compassion' (*eusplanchnos*),[15] words particularly pertinent to close kinship relationships and obligations. We are a Christian family. The fact that human beings have a common ancestry ties all of us to an equality based on kinship, and therefore, we inhabit a natural communitarian arena resting on a common spiritual ancestry as well as a common faith. Unlike worldly notions of community, where each member gives something of themselves, in a Christian community, God demands all of each of us and asks us to be wholeheartedly committed to others. For broken, wilful, sinful human beings, this has all too often proved to be rather problematic.

While the importance of the salvation of the individual person was a key understanding of the Dutch political, Calvinist theologian, and academic, Abraham Kuyper, he also saw the individual as not designed to remain in isolation but to be incorporated, not into a society, but wholeheartedly into a "covenant grace" community as already quoted: "The confession of particular, personal grace is untrue and unscriptural unless it arises within the context of the *covenant*."[16] Speaking of the voluntary, chosen kinships that provide a "living bond between human spirits . . . that has grown out of the root of Christ", the claim was made that these formed "the true connection between souls."[17] Kuyper saw that in our inter-connectedness we are not simply a "heap of souls on a piece of ground" but given Body life together by the Spirit.

> While the biblical descriptive ideal of a metaphorical body has spiritual appeal, as well as mandate, Church history has shown that the human participants in the metaphor fall far short of the incarnational, relational ideal. This is evident not only within the confines of ecclesiastical structures but of the Church writ large in the world—including in those institutions that practice Kingdom ministry through education and the church. The relationships in Christian community must have voluntarily "grown out of the root of Christ . . . . and a communal life can only develop by a route which neither steals the claims of freedom nor maintains a false unity."[18]

Communities of practice

The redemptive task to which we have been called, carrying our Christ's work by the empowering of His Holly Spirit, therefore demands a demonstration to the world of

---

¹⁵ Jobes, 2009
¹⁶ Kuyper, Ballor, Grabill, Kloosterman, Van & Mouw, 2016, p. 2–3
¹⁷ Kuyper & Bratt, 1998, p. 39
¹⁸ Ibid, p. 39

living in harmony, in community, and in fraternal love. These demonstrate to the world the potential of a transformed culture embodying a love-grounded civilisation: "By this everyone will know that you are my disciples, if you love one another" (John 13:35).

The idea of initiating and planning the functioning of such communities that are, or should be, rather self-generating and unstructured, is not a simple matter. Étienne Wenger, author of *Communities of Practice: Learning Meaning and Identity* pioneered the idea of communities of practice in the business world, with an obvious emphasis on the things people *do* together. Wenger's definition includes participation in solving recurring problems and developing a communal memory together. While at times aligning his idea of community more with our understanding of society, Wenger further explains:

> A community of practice is different from a network in the sense that it is "about" something; it is not just a set of relationships. It has an identity as a community, and thus shapes the identities of its members. A community of practice exists because it produces a shared practice as members engage in a collective process of learning. People belong to communities of practice at the same time as they belong to other organizational structures. In their business units, they shape the organization. In their teams, they take care of projects. In their networks, they form relationships. And in their communities of practice, they develop the knowledge that lets them do these other tasks.[19]

One way that these communities of practice differ from other groupings of people, is that while they are comprised of people who simply work or do things together, they will define their enterprise differently. Wenger used the illustration of two stone masons cutting stone—one working under the idea that he is cutting a nice, square stone, and the other that he is part of a project to build a cathedral. The difference between a group undertaking tasks as a society and one as a community of practice within a society is in how each imagines its work. In some ways, this is similar to David Brooks' idea when he wrote of two imaginary mountains that we climb. The first is claimed to build the individual, the second builds community:

> If the first mountain is about building up the ego and defining the self, the second mountain is about shedding the ego and losing the self. If the first mountain is about acquisition, the second mountain is about contribution. If the first mountain is elitist—moving up-the second mountain is egalitarian—planting yourself amid those who need, and walking arm in arm with them. You don't climb the second mountain the way you climb the first mountain. You conquer your first mountain. You identify the summit, and you claw your way toward it. You are conquered by your second mountain. You surrender to

---

[19] Wenger, 2018, para. 18

some summons, and you do everything necessary to answer the call and address the problem or injustice that is in front of you. On the first mountain you tend to be ambitious, strategic, and independent. On the second mountain and you tend to be relational, and restless.[20]

To further illustrate an approach to the two mountains, Brookes relates the following:

> In their book *Practical Wisdom*, psychologist Barry Schwartz and political scientist Kenneth Sharpe tell a story about a hospital janitor named Luke. In the hospital where Luke worked, there was a young man who'd gotten into a fight and was now in a coma, and he wasn't coming out. Every day, his father sat by his side in silent vigil, and had done so for six months. One day, Luke came in and cleaned the young man's room. His father wasn't there; he was out getting a smoke. Later that day, Luke ran into the father in the hallway. The father snapped at Luke and accused him of not cleaning his son's room.
>
> The first-mountain response is to see your job as cleaning rooms. "I did clean your son's room," you would snap back. The second-mountain response is to see your job as serving patients and their families. It is to meet the needs at a time of crisis. That response says, This man needs comfort. Clean the room again.[21]

Communities that exist and give meaning to members require, therefore, not only things that are 'done' together, but an imagining of the tasks and the way the tasks are to be carried out. In the practice and the imagining together of second mountain practice, rich, shared meaning is developed.

The creation of communities

In some ways, communities, as we understand the term here, form readily due to our human disposition to be in relationship with others, and for a wide range of reasons, such as cooperatively achieving some relationship goal, or simply the comfort of being with people who 'think like me' or have common interests. Ease of formation is also due to communities not usually requiring deep relationships, like collectives, communes, or specific relational structures, like societies. The aggregation of individuals in loosely structured communities, as we have seen, may be accomplished by providing some common "space" (for example, a hobby) that is desired in common by enough individuals. Of course, the dissolution of a community may be accomplished by the introduction of conflicting or competing goals.

---

[20] Brookes, 2019, p. xvi
[21] Ibid, pp. xiv–xv

It should be noted that the goals of a community are very different from the goals of societies or organisations. A community need not be striving towards a particular external vision to achieve something synergistically. Goals are more internal to the community: more about the feeling of togetherness with those with similar values and beliefs, and where caring love is expressed and accepted. Individual identity is not lost, though it is necessarily compromised to some extent as there will always be the ubiquitous, individualistic desire to be 'me', to be the 'captain of my own destiny', or to seek power.

Mimesis

When confronted or presented with new information, human beings tend to exhibit what has been called 'confirmation bias'. We more readily accept information that confirms what we already believe or assume, and that information affirms our beliefs and also our self-definition. The claim is made, however, that our connection with others goes even deeper than this. Mimesis, as described by René Girard[22] applies to a range of human relational frameworks but is included here with regard to the establishment and maintenance of community. Mimesis, Girard claimed, is the human inclination to mimic the desires of others. We can see this with young children as a child suddenly desires to play with a toy their sibling has picked up. Perhaps we have observed ourselves as we decided that we wanted something when we saw that someone else wanted it. We see this played out constantly as the force behind most advertising. We are also able to identify it as we observe humans interacting and coming together in the voluntary formation of a community, with loosely agreed-upon ideas or ideals and the desire to be a part of, or identify with, the group.

In teaching and learning interfaces within organisations, mimesis plays a crucial role. The 'teacher' in educational institutions, churches, or other organisations, because of their actual or metaphorical position in front of those who are learners, is able to express desires that may be mimicked. These may be communicated verbally or within the 'hidden' curriculum of body language and similar, subtle ways. This allows students, or draws students in, to mimic the desires. Positively, the mimicked desires would relate to such things as a desire to learn or a desire to know God more. Negatively, of course, there are always those who would deliberately or accidentally communicate alternate desires, such as those that lead away from positive learning experiences or towards those that are deleterious regarding a relationship with God.

In mimetic theory, however, there is another negative side, and a very significant problem arises when two people, or two groups of people, have the same object of desire and where the attaining of that desire is restricted to only one or the other. We

---

[22] Girard, 1986

see an illustration of this when desire becomes acquisitive in the legendary fight in the store over the very last desired toy (or, in COVID times, the last roll of toilet paper!). So, mimetic desire may cause competition, for which Girard used the term 'mimetic rivalry' as the desire being mimicked simultaneously becomes the obstacle to desire fulfilment. It is also the case that within a community context, the perceptions of each person or group for the desired object and the means to its attainment may be different, and this also creates conflict. Proffitt quotes René Girard as writing: "Paradoxically, when mutual love is absent, the only sentiment that can reconcile human beings is its opposite, a common hatred."[23] The power of human individual or group self-interest is substantial, as we know, and as the sociologist Theodor Adorno has said, cynically, though unfortunately, accurately, "the totality of society is maintained not by solidarity but by the antagonistic interests of human beings, by its antithesis."[24] This human tendency certainly mitigates against the maintenance of community.

These conflict points may even lead to 'mimetic violence'. Illustrations of this are common in history and may be seen in the desire of Cain and Abel to present sacrifices. Direct intervention against another party may not always be appropriate or available, so for Girard, another key factor in mimetic rivalry is the use of scapegoating: "the same force that divides people by mimetic rivalry also unites them by the mimetic unanimity of the scapegoat."[25] The scapegoat,[26] perhaps an arbitrary victim, is used as the object, perhaps of violence, to avoid violence between the mimetic rivals. Girard took as an illustration a perspective on John the Baptist's confrontation with Herod. We could imagine that there would have been some competition between Herod and his brother Phillip, regarding Herodias. In this scenario, John the Baptist becomes the scapegoat. While we may not agree with all of Girard's ideas regarding violence and scapegoat sacrificing in Scripture, including his view of the Cross, we do see many examples around us of scapegoating being used. This common use of scapegoating may be a means by which a form of guilt assuaging by atoning sacrifice is made, but it is also a significant means by which communities can become more united. The threat to unity involving guilt or conflict between two parties has been covered. Interestingly, the scapegoat may be a member of a conflicting party or perhaps even a random individual who is chosen by some means, and perhaps even unconsciously, becomes a surrogate, sacrificial victim. Scapegoating, and its concomitant psychological and

---

[23] Proffitt, 2016, p. 17

[24] Adorno, 2000, p, 44

[25] Girard & Freccero, 1986, p. 196

[26] The term scapegoat may be found in Leviticus 16: **21** "He [the priest] is to lay both hands on the head of the live goat and confess over it all the wickedness and rebellion of the Israelites— all their sins—and put them on the goat's head. He shall send the goat away into the wilderness in the care of someone appointed for the task."

emotional damaging of another human being, is not a biblical approach and not recommended, but it is all too common.

For community formation and maintenance, the issue of mimetic desire is significant, and we see many human groups divided over competing desires. This is particularly problematic when personal acquisitiveness is focused on a desired context or goal: it becomes a form of coveting. When an individual, or sub-group of zealots, lays claim to some goal, or way forward, as their own, not only is discord sown, but it may be that the others in the community abandon the originally shared ways forward altogether, resulting in the dissolution, or faction fracturing, of the community (c.f., the formation of denominations, etc.). As Girard noted, the same people who may be willing to fight together for a particular common-belief context can quickly turn to fighting against each other.

This is not so much of a problem where the group has a broad base: having a wide range of beliefs, ideals, values, and ideologies, and so on, around which the group may cohere. This will provide a situation with a better chance of keeping everyone happy, though, at the same time, everyone will also be somewhat dissatisfied. But if group members are willing to sacrifice their desire for what they may see as a group strongly united over their perceived orthodoxy for the sake of peace, then a level of co-existent harmony can prevail. The pain or discomfort of sacrifice can be mitigated also by reducing the strength, or watering down, of the base. We see this frequently in communities, from very small groups to global, ecumenical organisations such as the World Council of Churches. Apart from the problem of there being usually a degree, perhaps minor, of dissatisfaction on the part of group members, it is often difficult for the community to move ahead towards a particular consensus.

Strangely, community is not about leadership!

Questioning whether a community may be led may appear, perhaps, as a radical idea. Under the definitions we are using for community and community relationships, however, it may be argued that **a community cannot be led** in the sense that, for example, a society or a commune may be led. This relies on the argument that communities are joined voluntarily, their rather amorphous nature, and the primary purpose of community is to relate—not to "do" something or "go" somewhere necessarily. Where there emerges leadership in a community, either naturally or by the design of some individual, this will exert some form of influence or control over the group, giving direction and group purpose, and for the community, there will be a risk of devolving into a society. No longer would members bond for the sake of bonding, but other purposes and structures will inevitably begin to appear, and under these, interpersonal relationships will change in direction and intensity—quantitatively and qualitatively. Also, communities, or what we might term pure communities, or ideal communities, are defined by their practice of informal and assumed shared agency—that is, where everyone is sharing equally any choices and consequences that may arise. This naturally accepted system is damaged when a leader becomes a decision-maker and consequence-setter.

Some time ago, my wife and I published a slightly tongue-in-cheek article on the concept of 'leadership' titled, "A redefinition of leadership: What on earth did we think we were doing?"[27] In the article, we looked at the fact that the term 'leadership' comes to us 'fully loaded' with a range of meanings, and most of these have their origins in the Enlightenment, the Industrial Revolution, and modern management theories. As involved as we all are in the West in a variety of groups, we do not question the necessity for leadership. It just is, and we work to make it function more effectively. The literature pertaining to the subject is enormous, as thousands of authors, researchers, and theoreticians have tried to make sense of the concept and apply their perspectives to practical situations. A WorldCat search for English books published since 1950 with 'leadership' in the title, showed over 120,000 results, and this includes thousands by Christian writers. Conferences and seminars are conducted around the theme, and universities run degree courses related to it. So, why do we think leadership is such an important topic? Despite the Christian literature and teaching on leadership, the word is almost non-existent in the Bible. In the NIV translation, there are 2 references in Numbers and one in Psalms, which is later quoted in Acts. The Old Testament references use Hebrew words other than 'leadership' as we might understand it, and the New Testament reference is to a Bishop or overseer. One might think that something that we find so essential to thinking about groups of human beings relating and working together would have some prominence in the Bible. Instead, the Bible uses a range of different terms that sometimes become clumped together under our modern Western idea of leadership. The terms used for 'leadership' roles may include apostle, priest, king, overseer, shepherd, anointed one, elder, prophet, and so on. None of these gifts to the Church or nation is exactly what would be defined in terms of, for example, a 'leader' of an educational institution, though there are elements to which frequent reference is made.

There appear to be significant reasons why the Bible does not treat the subject with the same attention we might give it today, and these point to relationship frameworks. First, the Bible uses some terms for positions that apply to aspects of what we term leadership and in particular those linked in the New Testament to the establishment of the early Church. Despite this, most of these may refer to management rather than the vision, mission, values, and direction setting that we may envisage of leaders today. Elders, deacons, pastors, and others held positions with some degree of authority in

---

[27] Beech & Beech, 2016

the emerging organisational structure of the Church. The new society, the Church, made up of fallen human beings, required some level of regulation—rules and governance. From a biblical perspective, however, these leaders were, and are today, to be merely secondary leaders under the all-encompassing leadership of Christ. He is the leader. He is the authority. He is the judge. He is the One to set vision, mission, and determine values and directions. And, as so much of the Old Testament points towards, and the New Testament declares, He is the King.

Instead of seeing the Bible as only being about *us* and about God's communication with *us*, we might try to see it as God communicating through His Creation and taking direct action to guide human authors to write down His commentary. In this light, we can see that the biblical narrative has much to do with God's relationship with His Creation, and in particular His image bearers, and His concern for the relationships the image bearers have with each other. Throughout history, up until the establishment of the Church, God made relational covenants a number of times. These could be with individuals, families, tribes, or a nation, but they could have a force for many generations. The covenant God made with Israel through the giving of the Law on Mount Sinai did include lists of rules and regulations, but this, of course, was only a temporary covenant until the New Covenant was established in Christ. Under Moses, Joshua, and others, the new nation of Israel required an organisational structure to form a functioning, cohesive society.

We might say, then, that there can be an agreement, such as a constitution, for example, that sets out how we must live and live together, but in Christ, we do not have a constitution. Instead, we have a bonding, relational covenant. Under this New Covenant, God desires His image bearers to relate together, not as society members (requiring earthly managers and leaders), but as community members, sharing together the calling and vision of their God; as members of a collective, a family with Christ at the centre; as a commune, seeking deep relationships together and with Christ, the commune Shepherd. While it may be useful, and even necessary, for groups within the universal Church to have some form of organisational or societal structure, that is not the fundamental way God desires us to relate. Under-shepherds (pastors) have a primary role, not in organising, but in feeding and caring for the needs of the flock. God's priority was always covenant, and the bonding was always to be love-based rather than law-based. That being the case, the Bible has no need to emphasise our Western concepts of leadership; instead, it emphasises Christ as King, and those who are bound in love to Him. So, community and leadership, as we tend to understand them, do not play together on the same field. Instead, leadership implies some level of structure, of organisation, while community denotes trusting, caring, and loving interpersonal relationships between group members.

6. Collective

The self-system consists of three fundamental components: the individual self, the relational self, and the collective self. All selves are important and meaningful and all are associated with psychological and physical health benefits. However, the selves are not equally important and meaningful. We propose a three-tier hierarchy of the motivational potency of the self-system, with the individual self on top, followed somewhat closely by the relational self, and followed distantly by the collective self.[1]

A number of cultures have been described in very general terms as being collectivist, and this defining feature is indicated in their prioritising of collectivity in their relationship frameworks. In this sense, cultures such as a number of those found in Latin America, Asia and the Middle East may spring to mind as they have been referred to as collectivist cultures.[2] At the same time, while there will be elements of individualism, societism, and communitarianism, in a collectivist culture, some or all of the unique features of collectivity may be observed and researched. As discussed below, not all collectivist cultures, or subcultures, are the same, but there are commonalities. As with the other components of the relationship framework series, extreme or 'pure' collectivism may be purely theoretical. While this may be the case, as you read this chapter, you will be able to recognise collectivist traits within groups with which you work or of which you are a member.

Due to the implications of procreation, collectivism,[3] or humans relating in tight groups, is a relational structure that is common to most, if not all, cultures and sub-cultures to some degree, even in the individualistic West (including in Christian organisations and institutions). It seems that all human beings like the idea of being a part of an ingroup and consider others to be distinct from them as members of outgroups.[4] Within postmodern individualism, the human 'group' effectively might be said to be one person, but for strong, cultural collectives, it is a group structured around a significant core. It is difficult for Westerners to really appreciate just how powerful this concept may be in the worldview and practice of those in strongly collectivist cultures.

---

[1] Sedikides, 2002, p. 236
[2] Lui & Rollock, 2018; Muller, 2000
[3] Sometimes referred to as familism
[4] Triandis, 1995

The most significant defining features of collectivities include ingroups, outgroups, ingroup structure, honour and shame, and issues of trust. These factors are worth considering, not only in terms of other cultures, but for our own institutions and organisations. It may make it easier for us to be able to see collectivist features in our organisations if we can identify them in collectivist cultures where they are much more clearly defined.

Collective ingroups

In a collectivist culture the core group is comprised mostly of family-centric ingroups where other family groups are considered to be outgroups. (In subcultures such as those we find in our organisations and institutions, the ingroup may not be a family, but similar groupings may form.) Generally, at a cultural level, an ingroup is something into which one is born. Life is lived for the benefit and honour of the ingroup, though there may also be strong self-interest. This strongly influences decision making as seen in the illustration given earlier of the Bolivian girl needing to consult her family before making a decision for Christ. So, in collectivist cultures, "Groups and societies shape the fate of individuals; individuals have value to the extent that they appropriately fulfil their place and role within their relational network and should be sensitive to contextual factors that determine their fate".[5] The self-concept of the individual is therefore seen in terms of group characteristics rather than individual ones.[6] That said, the role of the individual may be quite strong in collectivism, particularly as it is usually as an individual that each member engages with those in outgroups. Rather than the somewhat homogenous relationality in communitarianism, the essence of collectivism is the wide range of strong positive and negative relationships in which an individual may be embedded.

As Westerners, and observing from a distance, we may see collectivist cultures as being one large collective unit, but, in fact, the opposite is the case, and this is an important distinction to make. Collectivist cultures at a national level are comprised of a *collection of ingroup collectives*, although it may be possible for a society to form a type of single, ingroup, collective. The core of each ingroup collective in these cultures generally will be the head of the family, then the immediate family, members of which will be tightly bonded to the core. These are stronger bonds than those encountered in groups in individualistic societies. The further an individual lies from the locus of the head of the family, or the nuclear family core, the weaker the bond. From the nuclear family, close, then more distant blood relatives, then others, such as godparents, lie towards the periphery. Beyond these, and much more loosely connected to the core,

---

[5] Oyserman, 2015, p. 4
[6] Jagers & Mock, 1995

there may be work colleagues or special friends, but often these are only invited to the edge of the ingroup if there is some perceived advantage from the relationship.

The bonding within the collective provides a level of group harmony, solidarity, and protection, and there is a reluctance to introduce what might appear to be extensive 'fraying around the edges' of the collective. A feature of the collectives, however, is that in order to improve the prestige of the collective (to bring honour to it), and hence of the individual members, relationships will be developed with outsiders. These relationships are fostered as part of a natural *quid pro quo* obligatory system. To take an example from the classed society in Bolivia, a family may invite someone of higher social standing to the birthday party for their child, or to a family barbecue, with the expectation that the invitation would be reciprocated. Once this level of relationship has been developed, the family will feel freer to ask favours of the one who is further up the social scale and therefore has more influence.[7]

One of the significant features of ingrouping that has been mentioned is that it implies the existence of outgroups—all other ingroups in the culture— and they are to be treated differently.

> In collectivist cultures people share and show harmony within ingroups, but the total society may be characterized by much disharmony and nonsharing, because so many interpersonal relationships are individual—outgroup relationships. For instance, if the ingroup is defined as "family and friends and other people concerned with my welfare" (Triandis, 1972), then most relationships with merchants, policemen, government bureaucrats, and so on are outgroup relationships.[8]

An extreme, though very common, feature of outgroup-ness we may see in many cultures is ascribing a defining label to another group and thus defining them as 'other'. Such speech acts of othering by reclassification (for example, claiming that a particular group of human beings 'are animals') may be done in order to reject, overpower, or attack with claimed impunity and clear conscience.[9] This may result in extreme measures, as Drakulic claimed: "Once the concept of 'otherness' has taken root, the

---

[7] Beech, 2019

[8] Triandis, Bontempo, Villareal, Asai & Lucca, 1988, pp. 325–326. (One sees at times instances where a church is formed by those from different countries from a region noted for its collectivist culture. It is not unusual for such churches to disintegrate as the different country groups will see others as outgroupers.)

[9] Othering, or in its extreme form, dehumanizing implies declaring another human being to be "not my kind". It may be at the level of "not my kind of person", to "not my kind of race", to "not my species". This is the foundation of racism and xenophobia. In its strongest, other species, version, the claim usually morphs to "monster"—something that is not understood, is to be feared, and something that must be destroyed.

unimaginable becomes possible."[10] There have been so many examples of this through human history, though we think particularly of war situations where othering would seem to be an essential part of conflict. A tragic example of this was the attacks of the Hutu militias against the Tutsis in Rwanda in 1994 when it was reported that up to a million people were killed. Waghid and Smeyers wrote that the indoctrination that had facilitated the killing and other atrocities was as a result of othering: "They call the Tutsi 'inyenzi', which means cockroaches, in other words insects that have to be destroyed."[11]

At a less violent level, due to the "family/relationship primacy", Schwartz et al.[12] commented that actions which may not be permissible within the ingroup may be perfectly permissible to do to the outgroup. Collective ingroup members may feel, not only that it is permissible, but even feel a moral obligation to their ingroup, to steal from, cheat or lie to, members of an outgroup. This moral dualism is evidenced in the individual's speech and actions relating to the two groups.

Understanding that there may exist what we may perceive to be these elements of moral dualism in collectivist cultures can be useful for those from the West wishing to do business with those in collectivist cultures. Decision-making within collectivist contexts relies much more on relationships and the collectivist worldview than might be the case in individualistic cultures. The deeming of the 'right thing to do' is strongly influenced by the relational ingroup/outgroup contexts. Referencing Chinese culture particularly, Gambrel and Cianci found that the hierarchy of needs developed by Maslow within a Western, individualistic context did not reflect a collectivist model accurately: "In a collectivist culture, the basic need is belonging; self-esteem is eliminated, and self-actualisation is attained in terms of meeting societal development needs."[13]

This attention to the ethical demands of the core group vis-à-vis an outgroup has been well illustrated through history and applies not only to what have been called collectivist cultures. All cultures are capable of containing some collectivist elements. On a smaller scale than inter-country war, the collectivisation of denominational groups with the othering of those from a different denomination has also led to many abuses through history, and many continue today. These have included martyrdom in many instances, torture, and inquisitions, and numerous wars supposedly over religious beliefs. To take a further dramatic example from Church history:

> In Prague, May, 1618, a tense meeting was held between Catholic leaders and those from the Protestant, Bohemian estates. The recorder of the meeting

---

[10] Drakulic, 1993, p. 3
[11] Waghid & Smeyers, 2012, p. 12
[12] Schwartz et al., 2010
[13] Gambrel & Cianci, 2003, p. 143

described the tension ending in physical conflict which involved the defenestration [throwing out of a window] of three of the Catholic group—all of which somehow survived the twenty-meter fall. During the meeting, in response to a strongly worded letter supposedly from the Catholic monarch, a strongly worded response was read. It referred to the original letter that claimed that the Protestant lives and honor were forfeit and continued: "We came to a unanimous agreement among ourselves that, regardless of any loss of life and limb, honor and property, we would stand firm, with all for one and one for all."[14]

The mention of honour in this example is significant. Collectivist cultures have often been referred to as shame or honour cultures,[15] though the collectivist cultures of Asia are sometimes referred to as 'face' cultures[16], where shame is equated (though not exactly) with losing face. The collectivist concept of group embeddedness contrasts with the Western individualist stance on the autonomy of the self. This embeddedness and the bonds that produce it are of high value to the collective member and must be preserved. Otherwise, shame or loss of face is incurred. While guilt in the West may be seen as one's judgement on one's actions, shame is the sense of the judgement of others on one's actions and in a highly relational culture the sense of shame, of bringing shame on oneself or on the ingroup, may be very strong indeed. We see examples of this in Asian cultures, where students who fail examinations may commit suicide, or commentators may lie openly in the media to promote honour or limit shame for their ingroup or culture.

Honour and shame

The honour-shame pair was highlighted by Ruth Benedict[17] in her studies in Japan following World War II, when comparing North American and Japanese cultures. In a tight relational structure, where the individual is defined to a large extent by the ingroup relationships, "shame can be seen as a signal of a threat to the bond"[18] and is to be avoided at all costs. In the Orient, we see that the idea of the individual without reference to others becomes meaningless, and the perspectives and reactions of those of significance in one's ingroup take priority over all else. Writing from an Asian perspective, Yau-Fai Ho wrote:

> While it is not a necessity for one to strive to gain face, losing face is a serious matter which will, in varying degrees, affect one's ability to function effectively in society. Face is lost when the individual, either through his action or that of people

---

[14] Heifferich, 2009, p. 16
[15] House et al., 2004; Hofstede, 1984; Triandis, 1995; Muller, 2000; Blaschke, 2001
[16] Wu, 2013
[17] Benedict, 1946
[18] Scheff, 2003, p. 239

closely related to him, fails to meet essential requirements placed upon him by virtue of the social position he occupies.[19]

As mentioned, not all collectivities are structured or function in the same way. While there are elements of shame and honour being highlighted in them, the form this takes varies. Uskul, Oyserman and Schwarz, for example, compared the Chinese, Confucianist collectivism with its focus on "harmony-modesty, fitting in, not sticking out, and not bragging"[20] with the more overt honour-seeking that may be found in the Mediterranean region, Latin America, some areas in Africa, and in the Middle East. In making this contrast, they wrote:

> Within a culture of honor, the central collective dimension is maintaining a good reputation—both within the group and with regard to relationships with outgroups. Like Confucian-based cultures of modesty, cultures of honor are collective— groups and group membership matter and reputation is both gained and lost not only through one's own actions, but also through the actions of others with whom one is closely associated (typically kin but also other social groupings). Because cultures of honor are collective in focus, it is likely that at least some of the literature on cognitive consequences of collectivism is generalizable beyond East Asia.[21]

This necessary ethical stance may be seen within the *guanxi* network of relationships in China.[22] The focus of these relationships between individuals is not fixed on any particular individual but on the particular nature of the relations between individuals who interact with each other. The focus is placed upon the relationship."[23] The strength of this concept in Chinese culture is so strong that, according to Leung and Wong,[24] it has even become embedded in Confucian philosophy, and its study has coined the term *guanxiology*.[25] The characteristics of *guanxi* relationships were said by Buttery and Wong[26] to include: Trust (respect, know others); favour (loyalty, obligation); dependence (harmony, reciprocity); and adaptation (patience, cultivation). These characteristics are inculcated within the culture over time, and they provide the foundation for what has been termed an "ethics of shame".[27] This has been contrasted by Ruth Benedict and others[28] with Western individualistic cultures where, as mentioned, guilt, disapproval in one's own eyes, is often of more importance than shame, disapproval in the eyes of one's ingroup.

---

[19] Yau-Fai Ho, 1976, p. 867
[20] Uskul, Oyserman & Schwarz, 2010, p. 192
[21] Ibid., pp. 192–193
[22] Gold, Guthrie, & Wank, 2002
[23] King, 1985, p. 63
[24] Leung & Wong, 2001
[25] Man & Cheng, 1996
[26] Buttery & Wong, 1999
[27] Aldrich, 1939
[28] For example, Harris, Wolgrave, & Braithwaite, 2004

The behavioural outworking of shame in the face of the collective may be seen in collectivist cultures where individuals are removed, for one reason or another, from the collective, primarily, the family. If there is a perceived limited possibility of the members of the family seeing or hearing news regarding an individual's behaviour, then the collective-required moral constraint is removed, and shameful behaviour may more readily occur. University students who live in a distant city, for example, may be prone to drunken behaviour, drug taking, and other actions that would not be permitted at home due to the shame it would incur. Of course, we see this also in Western cultures, where there remains a form of collectivism in groups of people even while living in the midst of individualism, but the contrast between the two situations appears to be starker in collectivist cultures.

We also regularly see examples in the news of instances or examples of ingroup/outgroup issues in collectivist cultures. To take one example, years ago, during the USA's "shock and awe" campaign in Iraq, as international news coverage showed the devastation in the country, Mohammed Said al-Sahhaf, the Iraqi Information Minister, was seen explaining to the world on television that, "Iraq will not be defeated, Iraq has now already achieved victory—apart from some technicalities."[29] He would have known that that was not true, indeed, very far from the truth, and yet he boldly proclaimed it to the world because his point had nothing to do with truth and lies as we might see in the West, but with honour and shame. He was duty-bound to lie. It was his moral obligation. For Sahhaf, saving face was imperative, and he was later quoted as saying, "I did my duty to the last minute."

This non-individualistic morality can create problems as Westerners engage with collective cultures. Is the other person telling the truth or preserving honour? Is a child lying to a teacher to protect their honour or that of their family? In each of these cases, the individual involved may feel totally morally justified and feel no guilt. This, obviously, is rather puzzling to Westerners.

....

As something of an academic aside, collectivist relationality in individuals in highly collectivist cultures has been found to apply not only to other people but to relationships between objects that may be conceived as sets. Mourey, Oyserman and Yoon offered groups of four objects to subjects from collectivist and individualist cultures saying they could choose two. After making their choice, the subjects were told that one of the ones they had chosen was no longer available. The individualists were happy to choose another, while the collectivists, preferred to choose none at all rather than break the original item relationship they had conceived. As Mourey, Oyserman and Yoon explained:

---

[29] Weissberg, 2004, p. 173

Though likely developed to highlight the meaning of social relationships, cultural mindsets carry over into non-social contexts. Thus, a collectivist mindset, creates a momentary attunement to the possibility of a relationship, such that people with collectivist mind-sets can and do create relationships among objects on the spot and are loath to break up these relationships . . . . Because people with a collectivist mind-set experience initial choices together as a relationship, they are not valued separately . . . . Our studies imply that an accessible collectivist mind-set would reduce willingness to accept some chosen policy options if others cannot be obtained, which would reduce compromise.[30]

Trust

Before examining trust in a collectivist framework, we may first consider it in general terms. Trust between human beings is essential for us to be able to properly assess the predictability of social interactions and may take generalised (people can be trusted in general) or particularised (only my kind of people can be trusted) forms. It is, however, as Uslaner put it, "the chicken soup of social life."[31] In a general sense, trust in another is the expectation that they will respond to situations in which both parties are involved in a manner that is predictable or in accordance with our expectations. Robinson describes trust as the "expectations, assumptions or beliefs about the likelihood that another's future actions will be beneficial, favourable or at least not detrimental."[32] Of course, one may 'trust' that someone will always cause one harm in any encounter, but, of course, 'placing one's trust in' someone is different.

Trust between individuals who voluntarily join groups provides a 'virtuous circle' in that there must be a level of trust in order to join the group, and once joined, camaraderie develops between like-thinkers, and further trust is developed. In weighing up the risks involved in joining a group, including the level of vulnerability that may be required, there must be a belief that no harm will come to one, or that any perceived cost associated with joining the group would be outweighed by the perceived benefits. This means that trust involves risk-taking, and global research on values has found that those from wealthy countries are more trusting than those from poorer countries, with the conclusion being drawn that the wealthy could afford to take more risks.[33]

While there may be something in this, the neuroscience and genetic evidence give us a different perspective. In particular, studies have been carried out involving

---

[30] Mourey, Oyserman & Yoon, 2013, p. 1620
[31] Uslaner, 2000, p. 569
[32] Robinson, 1996, p. 576
[33] Paunov, 2019

oxytocin, a hormone linked to human bonding and also serotonin, a hormone related to feelings of well-being and these are linked to trust.

Trust pervades human societies. Trust is indispensable in friendship, love, families, and organizations and plays a key role in economic exchange and politics. In the absence of trust among trading partners, market transactions break down. In the absence of trust in a country's institutions and leaders, political legitimacy breaks down. Much recent evidence indicates that trust contributes to economic, political, and social success. Little is known, however, about the biological basis of trust among humans. Here we show that the intranasal administration of oxytocin, a neuropeptide that plays a key role in social attachment and affiliation in non-human mammals, causes a substantial increase in trust among humans, thereby greatly increasing the benefits from social interactions.[34]

Lou and Han[35] found a positive link between mental health conditions, the genetic receptors for oxytocin, and collectivism and similar links were found by Chiao and Blizinsky[36] between collectivist cultures and the well-being hormone, serotonin. The studies of genes linked with the neuroreceptors for oxytocin in particular showed that they appeared to be stronger, or more prevalent, in collectivist cultures.

Ingroups and trust in collectivist cultures

While outgroup members usually will not be trusted,[37] knowledge sourced from outgroups is recognised and may be trusted and included, but only if it resonates with the knowledge of the ingroup or, ideally, can be used for the benefit of the ingroup. The closer an individual is to the core of the ingroup, the higher the level of trust afforded by the individual to that core and members of outgroups are often not to be trusted at all. Instead, they may "use avoidance behaviours, and compete with, manipulate, and exploit outgroups more extensively than individualists."[38] To cite examples from the Beech research relating to a collectivist culture:

> Héctor suggested that in terms of a complete (100%) trust, you could not even trust the person inside your own shirt! Christians may trust God 100%, and mothers, he said, could probably be trusted to about 90%. There is the feeling that "God . . . I may not understand but I will trust" and "Mum may lie to me but it is basically because she loves me and wants the best for me." In general,

---

[34] Kosfield, Heinrichs, Fischbacher & Fehr, 2005, p. 673
[35] Lou and Han, 2014
[36] Chiao & Blizinsky, 2010
[37] Muller, 2006
[38] Huff & Kelly, 2003, p. 83

Héctor felt that there were levels of trust that one had to have in relationships and these stayed in place until the trust was broken in some way.

In his small village [in South America], Hernando believed there was a high level of trust between family members and even extended family members. Between friends he said there was not much trust and this was a delicate area. The friend may or may not keep his or her word. In more general terms within the community Hernando cited *ayne* [exchange of work] as an example of an expression of trust and this relates to obligations and the fulfilling of one's word by complying with the obligation to act.[39]

Knowledge in collectives

The issue of trust has a strong impact epistemologically. This is due to what Royce and Smith[40] referred to as 'psycho-epistemological priorities'. They argued that there were four general sources of knowledge in which we place our trust, as truthful and reliable, and these are ranked in priority order differently for different cultures and individuals. The four they claimed were:

Rationalism: Where we place faith in evidence provided by reason or cognitive processes

Empiricism: Where we place faith in evidence provided by the senses

Intuitionism: Where we place faith in evidence provided by feelings and intuition, and includes revelation such as divine revelation, dreams, etc.

Authoritarianism: Where we place faith in the authority of an individual or individuals in positions of influence

For individualistic Westerners, priority is more likely to be given to empirical and rational evidence, but for collectives, the sure foundation for knowledge lies at the authoritative heart of the ingroup. Cultural knowledge is owned by the ingroup, and particularly by those near the core, and this knowledge is passed from generation to generation. Where new knowledge is sought within the group, for example, understanding and solving a problem, then the issue will be discussed at length, sometimes for a very great length, before coming to a unanimous decision and the incorporation of that knowledge into the group.

Knowledge may be imported from outside for utilitarian purposes, such as for the building up of, or gaining honour for, the individual and therefore for the ingroup.[41] Within modern, collectivist cultures, knowledge now comes from outside the group via

---

[39] Beech, 2011, p. 238

[40] Royce & Smith, 1964

[41] In South American countries, for example, many students going to university may wish to study undergraduate courses such as law or bio-chemistry because then they will be able to use the title, 'Doctor'—even if their reality means that to earn a living they may be driving a taxi.

many means such as print and audiovisual media, social media, and through schooling where members from a wide range of ingroups are 'forced' to mix and learn together. The provision of an effective education requires the formation of artificial collectivities in the form of class groups. Of course, if this process is particularly effective, the authoritative centre for knowledge becomes the classroom teacher, thus breaking, or at least placing stress on, the familial core structure.

Some Biblical perspectives

There are so many instances in the Scriptures that point to a collectivist way of thinking and relating, and it can be enlightening to identify these as we come across them in our Bible reading. By contrast, we might say that the development of theories pertaining to personal identity and fulfilment that are seen in the relationship category settings are usually grounded in naturalism or materialism. The missing element in these is the existence and activity of the Creator and Sustainer God of the Bible. Within the Judeo-Christian cultural tradition, individual and group identity and fulfilment should be derived first from a direct spiritual relationship with God. Throughout the Scriptures, we see multiple examples of the collectivist character of the groups of people described, and we see God's encouragement of His people to operate and relate as a form of collective, with Him as the essential core. That said, much of the Old Testament is devoted to descriptions and consequences of His people moving away and seeking another core. While there was a degree of unity under God at times, when we see in the Old Testament the Northern and Southern Kingdoms split following Solomon's reign, to become distinct ingroups, the animosity could be intense. This continued, and we see it again in the New Testament with the othering, or outgrouping, by the Jews of the Samaritans.

In the New Testament, there are many other examples of those who were seen as outgroupers, and for many, Jesus was seen as being more "outgroup" than any human could. The early believers also formed ingroups that stood in opposition to other ingroups of Jewish, Roman or Greek origins. The ingroup to which they were called was the "family of God", where the core of the ingroup was, and is, Christ. In this case, earthly family members may form a band a little further from the core: "Anyone who loves his father or mother more than me is not worthy of me; anyone who loves his son or daughter more than me is not worthy of me" (Matthew 10:37). The allegiance to the core, initiated and empowered by the Holy Spirit, has a uniting purpose.

The coming of the Gospel then, as now, caused a clash, not only of ideas or theories, but of deeply seated cultural ideologies, confronting the core of our relational systems and the fundamental and subconscious assumptions we have about everything. Perceived outgroupers, such as the Apostle Paul, came to groups of people whose god at their relational core was merely something that had been made in human or other image. The reaching out by Paul and others in what we might describe as missionary work was very purposeful and confrontational to reach what for them were outgroups.

The full name of the Greek god Zeus is Zeus Xenios—protector of strangers, or those from outgroups. We see in the New Testament in particular that God is the lover of strangers (see the separation of the sheep and goats in Matthew 25, especially the comments about the *xenos*/stranger). Contrasting with humanly devised collectivism, Jesus' perspective was that outgroupers were to be loved, as God, who is altogether 'other' to us, loves us. Complying with this command has always proved difficult for us, whether seen between groups (for example, denominations) or between 'cliques' within a single church, institution, or organisation.

Collectives in practice: Collectives as alternatives?

In Christian organisations, there may be some appeal for us to consider collectivism as an alternative to individualism, but as Archer has noted, "The opposite of individualism is not collectivism but fraternity."[42] Given our from-birth familism that naturally leads to a form of family-based collectivism, we do tend to migrate at times and in particular circumstances to a collectivist mode. Other factors, however, may also contribute to personal and cultural relationship proclivities. Educators know that it is commonly believed that we tend to give higher grades if we have a hot drink in our hand as we mark papers. Ambient temperatures have been thought to influence relationships and vice versa. Research in four studies by Ijzerman and Semin[43] found that the closer we are to people physically, the warmer we tend to feel, and we feel closer when exposed to warmer temperatures—even a hot drink. An extrapolation of the work of Ijzerman and Semin, which was drawn by Colzato, van Beest and van der Wildenberg, included an interesting possible theory:

> Interestingly, Italy and Israel are notoriously "warm" countries, conditions that in view of Ijzerman and Semin's observation might propagate both more collectivistic religions, like Roman Catholicism and Judaism, and behavior that takes other people more into consideration.[44]

While we may find such findings of some interest, research by Chablis et al., warned that while there had been research that seemed to indicate that holding a hot drink caused people to judge another's personality as being warmer, the size of the effect may be very small.[45] We can also see that there are, of course, examples of individualistic cultures that lie in warmer climates and collectivities that have formed in

---

[42] Arche, 2011, p. 20
[43] Ijzerman & Semin, 2009
[44] Colzato, van Beest & van der Wildenberg, 2010, p. 93
[45] Chablis et al., 2019

colder regions, so the point being made may be merely an interesting generalisation to ponder. But where does that leave us with regard to identifying collectives in our own back yard, so to speak?

Features we may recognise in collectives in any group in which we participate can include the following:

- The family often features as the essential structure for a collective
- Close adherence to, and love for, a 'core' person or small group
- The 'othering' of other groups
- Group bonding becomes strengthened by the declaration of a common enemy or enemies
- Lack of trust exists between groups
- Honour preservation is seen as important
- Due to the need to preserve honour, what others might consider to be 'sins' may not lead to feelings of guilt
- Shame is to be avoided, and if experienced, may be severe
- Nepotism or favouritism are common due to the trust extended to ingroup members and the distrust of others
- Ethical behaviour is determined by the core and particularly adhered to by those closest to the core
- Individuals who, for one reason or another, find themselves distant from the group will be less worried by shame before their group and can lose ethical and moral constraints
- Decision-making tends to be undertaken within the group and with the approval of the core rather than by individuals
- Key features of the knowledge of the collective are passed down through successive generations by the core

While there exist collectives within groups of human beings, be they Christian or otherwise, on a larger scale, denominations, churches, and education systems can also operate as collectives. No doubt, we are familiar with some of the features above in a range of Christian and other groups and at the level of Western culture, Christians have been seen, and are increasingly being seen, in collective terms as an outgroup from larger cultural groups. And, of course, we may see ourselves in this way as well. While within Western individualism, guilt has an important place, there will still be evidence of honour seeking and shame reducing. There are also problems relating to trust—between Christians and non-Christians—and in some cases, taking advantage of the others. Knowledge may not be judged to be held at the 'core' of a larger cultural group, such as a national culture, though in general terms there may be a figurative acknowledgement of 'scientists and technicians' holding this place, or even a constitution or other national documents. Within Christian groups, the knowledgeable core may be seen as the source of orthodox teaching. For Christians, the bridging of these group divisions has usually come under the heading of 'evangelism', but the difficulties posed appear to be increasingly greater as we have moved to modernism, and then post-modernism, and now beyond. Fortunately, the Holy Spirit has been tasked with convicting and convincing in ways we cannot.

Despite the fact that we may often see evidence of collectivism in Christian groupings, and we may see examples of it in the Scriptures, this speaks to the general human condition, fallen image bearers of God, rather than a template for Christian living and co-existing. Given the features listed above, we see that while God commands that His people live together in loving relationships, the structure of a Godly collective is to be substantially different. If we reexamine the features above, we are able to contrast a biblically grounded version with the version into which many cultures and subcultures fall. A more biblical version then, includes:

- While families are important, and critically so, we have Jesus' comment regarding the trusted core: "Anyone who loves his father or mother more than me is not worthy of me; anyone who loves his son or daughter more than me is not worthy of me." (Matthew 10:37)

- Close adherence to, and love for, the 'Core' where the Core is the Triune God who created us and all things, bringing us into close relationship with Him through the sacrificial death of Jesus the Christ, and sustaining our relationship with Him through the power of His Holy Spirit.

- A denial of self. Individualists, all too easily, are allegiant to ourselves, but a deep relationship with the Creator God means allegiance to Him and to Him alone.

- The 'othering' of other groups is to be handled with care. Others, non-Christians or those of other religious belief systems, may not be trusted fully and knowledge from them must be sifted to find Common Grace truth. However, they are not to be hated, abused, taken advantage of, or lied to. The 'othering' of other Christian groups in the worldly sense is forbidden. Others are to be loved.

- Group bonding is to be strengthened by strengthening the adherence and allegiance to the Core.

- Lack of trust will exist towards groups that do not have the same Core but they are to be respected and loved.

- Honour preservation is important, but it is God's honour that is sought, proclaiming His greatness to all.

- Guilt, our judging of ourselves to have done wrong, arises from the searching of our hearts before the God who forgives and expunges our sin and guilt.

- Shame is to be avoided, but the important shame that is felt is not so much from others within the collective having knowledge of wrongdoing, but before the God who sees all things and knows all things and who calls for repentance and relationship restoration.

- Nepotism or favouritism may exist in that there is a need to work with those whose allegiance is also to the Core, but fairness and love for others are to be demonstrably exercised at all times.

- Ethical behaviour is determined by God and directed through the Scriptures and the conviction of the Holy Spirit.

- We are to watch for individuals who move away from the Core and seek to bring them back into fellowship.

- God is to have the ultimate decision-making role, and we are to seek His guidance and revelation of the decisions He makes.

- As the paraphrase of St Augustine says, "All truth is God's truth." While transmitted or mediated by those who have gone before, knowledge is not to be owned by individuals or the collective. It is His. Living in God's ingroup, therefore, means looking to him for truth and doing whatever is necessary to maintain a close relationship with Him in order to be inspired constantly by His truth.

Creating collectives

The historical, collectivist cultural type comprised of collectives may be of the involuntary, family-centred type, but collectives in the West may also be created or formed out of existing individualist contexts or from loosely bonded communities or societies.[46] We find examples of these in all levels of human groups, and usually, we do not have to look far to see them in action. While much of the time we may see the close relational bonding of human beings as being a good thing, there are, however, significant downsides to created collectives. As we consider this, examples may be brought to mind from our experiences of groups of humans.

Unlike family-based collectives, larger-scale collectives created in societies do not have a headship that is inherited through generations, but someone, usually with a charismatic leadership personality, draws the collective ingroup together, and most members join voluntarily, as is the case with many cults. As a particular headship may not be inherited and therefore the collective has no, or limited, historical foundation, they tend to be ephemeral and may collapse or dissolve with the demise of the head. While they survive, however, the relationship bonds near the core may be very strong and often may involve close family members. The head of the ingroup has great authority in the group and is the trusted source of knowledge or truth. There is a degree

---

[46] The functioning of something like John Maxwell's Five Levels of Leadership, for example, may work towards the formation of a relational collective around a core (leader).

of isolationism where all those in outgroups are declared to be 'other' and the claimed truth of the 'others' is deemed to be lies or 'fake news'. Perceived lies against the head or the ingroup may be expected from an outgroup, but shame-inducing insults will bring a strong reaction. All ethical and moral considerations, therefore, are based on bringing honour and avoiding or limiting shame. Indeed, at times, the heads of these collectives may commit the most egregious acts, but as long as they are perceived to be bringing honour or kudos in some form, the behaviour is deemed by collective members to be acceptable or simply ignored. The outgroups may be lied to, cheated, or abused in some way, with impunity as long as the intent is to bring honour to the head and the group, or to reduce shame. Within the ingroup, decisions are made by the head, and those surrounding the head are not likely to make decisions on their own without reference to the head and those in the core group. Where they are not able to do this, the tight relational bonding is threatened, damaged or strained, and usually they are removed from the collective or at least from being close to the core in order to maintain the integrity of the group's structure. That said, for collective members in the individualistic West, especially those at the periphery of the collective, individualism will still be a defining factor, but it will often be subjugated to the ingroup norms.

One very important factor to be considered in the maintenance, or continuity, of collectives, on a small or very large scale, is that if they are to achieve any sort of longevity, they must not be 'person'-based. Instead, they must be, or become, 'role'-based. It is not a particular person who heads a collective in a collectivist culture; it is the 'father' or 'parent', and the role is passed on from generation to generation. Collectivities grown in individualistic cultures, therefore, must have very clearly-defined roles and titles. For churches, for example, it is not the present leader but the continuing pastorate or the priesthood, in schools it is the principalship, in colleges and universities it is the president or vice chancellor—regardless of who holds the role at any given moment.

To develop a long-standing collective, therefore, means that the person at the centre must move the allegiance and relationship structures from themselves to the role or position, though many, particularly those who are ego-driven, will find that particularly difficult to achieve. Allegiance to the role has very significant implications, naturally, for leadership transition or succession. If the collective bonding is to Wendy, and then, suddenly, Sally is to be the group head, the collective may dissolve fairly rapidly. In our individualistic cultures, this is problematic, where we stress the importance of the person. Titles can be useful, and we see this in the British habit, in days gone by at least, of referring to the principal of a school as 'Headmaster', rather than by their name, as is certainly the case in some school contexts. In churches, we often see a leader being referred to as Pastor, Deacon, or Bishop, and so on.

For collectivist leadership succession, and the 'passing on of the baton', the emphasis must be on the baton, not the individuals involved. If our fallen natures can be overcome enough to do this, there is a need to have the baton 'role' clearly defined and the definition, including the structure and function of relationships, accepted by all members of the collective. For self-centred individualists seeking power or self-aggrandisement, neglecting self in favour of the role can be difficult, and for many, this cuts across our traditional and institutional understandings of 'leadership', implying elevated personhood. The more recent conceptualisation of leadership as servanthood would also require some refining so that the role may be well defined and agreed upon in order for a servant leader to function and pass that leadership baton on to the next generation.

7. Communal Living

We live disaggregated lives. We are disaggregated physically, many of us living far from family and home base. We are disaggregated sociologically, many of us shuttling between contexts that don't touch one another, compartmentalized social and civic habits compounded now by online engagement. We are also disaggregated morally, the elites we once trusted to lead either offended by the idea that there could be a shared compass in pluralistic times, or themselves so corrupted in character and vision that it's hopeless to defer in their direction.

And so we resort to an ancient survival mechanism activated when fear is kicked up and identities of all kinds are under siege: Find your team and defend it. It's your only shot at significance and psychic sanity.[1]

We are all familiar with the unofficial motto of Switzerland that was popularised through Dumas' *The Three Musketeers*: "All for one; and one for all!"[2] In the phrase, we see individuals committed to a particular type of protective relationship. The musketeers depicted were individuals within a structured society, a small community with common values, an ingroup, and with members having a deep commitment to each other: a communal bond, as it were. It is a bond that promotes *we-ness* over *me-ness*, where members have an extended self-identity.[3] "There exists an emphasis on social bonds and mutual interdependence such that the good of the individual is closely intertwined with the good of the group."[4] The communal bonds discussed in this chapter and the next differ from the bonds in collectivism in that they are more homogenous, rather than 'thinning towards the edges'. As such, communalism may be conceived as being more like communitarianism but with stronger relational bonds. There are elements of 'communal relationships' within many, if not most, human groups, including Christian organisations, churches, and schools. This chapter is somewhat longer than the others because it contains some insights into the higher level of co-existing that God intends for His Church. Communality denotes a deeper level of sharing as we find in the words commune and communion. As we

---

[1] Snyder, 2020, paras. 6, 7
[2] Dumas, 1993, pp. 84 & 85
[3] Nobles, 1991
[4] Boykin, Jagers & Elison, 1997, p. 410

consider the features of communality in this chapter, we might reflect on our own relational groups and institutions, and whether communality is something we desire to see in them, or if it might be practicable in any way.

When we speak of communal, communalism, communality, or commune, in the West, we immediately begin to think of communism or the communes established during the hippy era, or perhaps the Kibbutzim in Israel. To make something of a distinction for the purposes of this discussion, communism, rather than involving voluntary membership, is generally seen as promoting a form of State-*imposed* communal existence. We might note a confusion of terms in that the formal structure of commune-ism, or imposed communality, in countries such as the old Soviet Union, was based on formal, state-defined collectives for economic purposes. As with most governments, the State in these cases lays claim to knowledge and dictates what and how it will be taught across its territory. Thus, the ideology behind economic communes eventually becomes embedded in the society as a whole. At least that is the aspirational goal.

By contrast, communalism, while relatively rare in Western societies in purer forms, is seen in the holistic, communal mindset and is typical of villagers in many parts of the developing world. It is seen, or should be, also in the "one body" vision that God has for His Church. As we will see in the next chapter, it is illustrated in the African terms such as *ubuntu* that indicate an "I am because we are"—a way of thinking that rejects an atomistic view of human beings and includes relationships between humans and the physical and non-physical domains as integral to a definition of being human. This provides not only a different relational framework, but also a different way of looking at the world. In the last chapter, the way collectivists see sets of objects was mentioned. Regarding communalist cultures, research has shown that while individualists tend to focus on individual, salient objects presented before them, those from communal cultures also see the relationships between objects and their background context.[5]

Communality

Communalism denotes awareness of the fundamental interdependence of people. One's orientation is social rather than being directed toward objects. There is overriding importance attached to social bonds and social relationships. One acts in accordance with the notion that duty to one's social group is more important than individual rights and privileges. Hence, one's identity is tied to group membership rather than individual status and possessions. Sharing is promoted because it affirms the importance of social

---

[5] Colzato, van Beest & van der Wildenberg, 2010

interconnectedness. Self-centeredness and individual greed are frowned upon.[6]

Communal group membership may be based on some form of forced or voluntary membership (e.g., hippy communes where members may join voluntarily or be born into the group), or where that which is held in common may be considered to be illegal in the culture (e.g., drug production and use). Many communal groups, however, appear to resonate more with biblical principles. We worship a God who seeks communion with His Creation and particularly with His *imago Dei*, and He instructed His image bearers accordingly (Romans 12; 1 Corinthians 12; Ephesians 4; 1 Peter 2, etc.).

Daffin, Tyler et al., defined communalism in similar terms and added a distinction regarding collectivism:

> For Moemeka (1998), collectivism is a cultural value that facilitates individual pursuits, particularly by having individuals come together and form an aggregate or collective that will serve to protect the rights of the individual group members seeking to purse their self-interests. Thus, for Moemeka, individualistic tendencies and goals lie at the core of collectivism. Communalism, on the other hand, embodies a social orientation toward the maintenance of the community and focuses exclusively on the welfare of the group rather than on the individual interests and goals of group members.[7]

True communality is very difficult for us, as Western individualists, to comprehend because for us, each individual is distinct, and usually, we cannot conceive of a way of thinking and living that significantly denies individuality. The anthropologist, Bird-David,[8] made the distinction between *individuals* and *dividuals*—those who see themselves as independent entities, and those who see themselves as integral to a holistic reality: one with others in the group and with all of Creation (c.f., *ubuntu*). Such a holistic, cosmological engagement requires deep indoctrination, typically from birth to age thirty in village contexts, as commune members are trained in all ways of life and lore. Such indoctrination may be deemed to be impossible to achieve in modern Western cultures, given our systems of education and the age range to which they cater. This does not mean, however, that the enculturation process does not exist. Rather than a family or a village undertaking the enculturation, in the West, we have families, schools, society, mass media, and social media, all contributing in fractured and often antithetical ways to an individual's enculturation.

---

[6] Boykin, Jagers & Elison, 1997, p. 411
[7] Daffin, Tyler et al., 2008, pp. 285
[8] Bird-David, 1999

The worldview assumptions of normality as being one with the cosmos and a holistic sociology that are inherent to village cultures do not rely on volition but are inculcated from birth. And, as the African proverb indicates, the responsibility for the inculcation is not restricted to parents or a schooling system: "It takes a village to raise a child." Van der Walt listed the characteristics of African communalism as: "communal self-respect", "interdependence", "survival of the community", "group assurance", "co-operation and harmony", "affiliation", and "shared duties".[9] (After spending years in South Africa and Kenya, Stuart Fowler[10] described his experiences living in Africa as having exposed him to "authentic communal life".) Within the limitations of individualistic, Western contexts, perhaps the closest approach to communality is through "developing true mutual 'Gemeinschaft-like' interpersonal relationships, not merely a contractual society, but a communal spirituality . . . and a culture of fraternity."[11]

Different cultures no doubt have different levels of relational engagement, but in the Dutch culture, perhaps the word *gezelligheid* is useful. This describes "a cozy, fun, quaint atmosphere of belonging, a meaningful togetherness",[12] or "a communal sense of coziness, conviviality, trust, joy, and connection."[13] As pleasant as this sounds, it might be noted that communal groups may not be insulated from conflict. The deep enculturation processes of communal living provide both a definition of the self but also a definition of the self-in-commune (c.f., *ubuntu* once more). While identity-defining communal groups may exist in harmony with the societies from which they have separated, or from which they become marginalised, if attacked, they may react strongly, just as individuals react when their self-definition is perceived to be assaulted.

Communality in Scripture

The concern many in the past, and present, have had for biblically grounded, deep relationships, applied particularly to those intra-Church, but we may be dismissive of other examples where groups function communally, but within which the enculturation has been to beliefs antithetical to the Gospel. This view of a communality that has fallen from God's purposes denies the totality of what God's relational purpose for His human beings was to be. That is, yes, we are to love others, but loving Him must be the context for that relationship (for example, John 13:34, 35; Romans 12:10; Romans 13:8, etc.). This also brings to mind the accounts of life in the early Church (Acts 2:42–46; 4:34–35). In Scripture, the recurring theme of living as one, is seen in the marriage command in Genesis 2:24 (to become "one flesh"), in Jesus' declaration of the most important

---

[9] Van der Walt, 1997, pp. 29–44
[10] Fowler, 2014
[11] Bahovec, 2015, p. 344
[12] Mirkmayer & Ruggeri, 2015, p. 29
[13] Kaemingk, 2018, n.p.

commandments (Matthew 22:36–40), and in his prayer that his disciples "may be one" as he was with the Father (John 17:11, 21, 22).

Often, however, those of us within the Church have had difficulty thinking outside an individualist model. Deitrich Bonhoeffer, in his *Sanctorum Communio*, or Communion of the Saints, used not only the Latin phrase but described a communality of the church (*kirchliche Gemeinschaft*) where a "divine-human community is built upon individual persons endowed with the Spirit."[14] The vision of the incorporation of the church as individuals bonded by and with God, and acting in harmony with His Spirit, while recognising individuality, was taken up by John Calvin in his discussion of the use of "the communion of saints" in the Apostles' Creed.

> Moreover, this article of the Creed relates in some measure to the external Church, that every one of us must maintain brotherly concord with all the children of God, give due authority to the Church, and, in short, conduct ourselves as sheep of the flock. And hence the additional expression, the "communion of saints;" for this clause, though usually omitted by ancient writers, must not be overlooked, as it admirably expresses the quality of the Church; just as if it had been said, that saints are united in the fellowship of Christ on this condition, that all the blessings which God bestows upon them are mutually communicated to each other. This, however, is not incompatible with a diversity of graces, for we know that the gifts of the Spirit are variously distributed; nor is it incompatible with civil order, by which each is permitted privately to possess his own means, it being necessary for the preservation of peace among men that distinct rights of property should exist among them. Still a community is asserted, such as Luke describes when he says, "The multitude of them that believed were of one heart and of one soul" (Acts 4:32); and Paul, when he reminds the Ephesians, "There is one body, and one Spirit, even as ye are called in one hope of your calling" (Eph. 4:4). For if they are truly persuaded that God is the common Father of them all, and Christ their common head, they cannot but be united together in brotherly love, and mutually impart their blessings to each other. [15]

However, communality in practice, while intimated, is not commonly identified in Scripture. Old Testament accounts frequently reference high-profile individuals such as kings, priests and prophets, though there are limited accounts of some 'ordinary' persons, their family and daily life in their towns and villages. God's elect Children of Israel, however, were to live as a nation, as a united people, sharing beliefs and practices. Due to the diverse geographical locations of the people, as well as the

---

[14] Bonhoeffer & Green, 2009, p. 36
[15] Calvin & Beveridge, p. 673

influence of the Fall, the uniting of all members into anything like a commune proved extraordinarily difficult and was exacerbated by the rebelliousness of the people. The prophet Malachi, among others, related God's grievances against Israel and the significance of the breaking of the covenant God had made with their ancestors to bind them to Him and to each other. In particular, God noted that male Israelites had been marrying women from other countries and cultures (c.f., the example of Solomon) and the consequent following of the wives' pagan practices (Malachi 2:10–16). The incorporation of members of another culture or group into a communal group, without 'conversion' to full allegiance to the commune, obviously can foment disintegration of the group and destroy any communality that may exist. (This, of course, is a key concern of Christian institutions today, and particularly fundamentalist groups, that may act out of a fear of contamination or loss of identity.)

Communal knowledge

Communal villages around the world, due to a range of environmental and historical factors, have tended to form teaching and learning in relative isolation. These groups, partly because of the presuppositions embedded in their thinking about truth and knowledge, exhibit the traits of communes rather than a community, that is, merely a collection of individuals. To take the African communal living settings as an example again, knowledge is not individually owned but corporately owned by all village members[16] and naturally, this renders a different perspective on knowledge and truth that may apply across a people group. In Francophone West Africa, for example, educators have written of a 'Négritude epistemology'—a way of thinking about knowledge and learning that is specific to black African cultures.[17]

In communal villages, the proprietary knowledge is not quite universally held in common, however, as there may exist individuals who, by birth or election, serve as spiritual leaders, having some form of "secret knowledge" derived, purportedly, from an external source (c.f., also the Gnostics of early New Testament times). (From a biblical perspective, the ownership of truth is neither the prerogative of individuals, nor for collectives, communities, or communes, but, rather, this is the domain of God alone.) In educational institutions, this conceptualisation of communalised truth may result in students and academics being mystified by a Western-influenced institution's insistence regarding plagiarism regulations: if truth is owned by all, why nominate an individual?

While the context of an isolated village may appear to be somewhat in a closed-loop stasis, knowledge-wise, in reality, communal knowledge morphs and evolves. In

---

[16] Miller, 2015
[17] Senghor, 1968

order to attain warrant, new knowledge proposals are presented to a truth justification process in meetings of village members. Questions are asked of the knowledge regarding the reliability of its source, evidential bases, verifiability, pertinence, and so on. "Oral tradition is a source from which new knowledge can be created through expansion or deletion, because it is received knowledge that has been tested through everyday life or trial-and-error experimentation, and is capable of further improvement."[18] Knowledge accretion in commune, or village, settings may also be illustrated from within an Australian context, where an example of the operation of a traditional law, or lore, system is seen in the process of adopting new rules for the community by the Yolngu Aboriginal people of East Arnhem Land. A new law is discussed at length in the group (for up to two years according to Trugden[19]) before the elders produce an artefact (such as a sacred, woven bag) to represent the new law. Community members then go to a waterhole for the ceremony in which the law is officially adopted.

> In this Ceremony the objects representing the law are held by the political leader of that clan/nation and he, together with all the people of that clan, go under the water to indicate that they are under the discipline, responsibility and protection of the law. No one is above the law![20]

This lengthy discussion and the mass self-baptism by all members of the clan are ways to ensure that the new law, or knowledge of how things should be done, is owned by all.

This form of the embedding of law, or communally held knowledge, while taking time, does not imply immutability. New and improved laws may be processed over time. Changing law, or lore, with cultural change is evident in the Scriptures also where, for example, as a theologian friend quipped, rather tongue in cheek, regarding the reshaping of the Commandments through the biblical narrative (for example Exodus 20 and Deuteronomy 5, to Matthew 5 and 22:37–38, Mark 10:19, Luke 18:20, to Acts 15:29 and Romans 13:9): "The Ten Commandments were not written in stone, you know!" Notwithstanding these modifications, significant changes arising from oral tradition may be accomplished through written accounts, and this is indicated in the importance given to the Torah scrolls referenced frequently in the Old and New Testaments.

Oral or written, we see in the Old Testament accounts that specific God-given knowledge was to be embedded deeply in culture and practised communally. From writing on door posts to deep memorisation, the communal essentials were to be

---

18 Gegeo & Watson-Gegeo, 2001, p. 64
19 Trugden, 2000
20 Commonwealth of Australia, 1998, p. 1334

shared across the nation and promulgated to future generations. (Sanctions for non-compliance could include removal from the commune by death or banishment.) Whether in biblical illustrations or in villages, the trans-generational dissemination of communal knowledge emphasises the role of 'ancestors' and their role in providing a tried and tested structure for each generation to live in conformity with the traditional, communal ways. Within communal societies, the narratives from the ancestors are repeated often, till absorbed, their symbols or totems are carved in wood or stone, and they are revered. By contrast, as Westerners, reading the genealogies of Jesus in Matthew 1 and Luke 3, as well as the lists of names commonly found in the Pentateuch, is usually something we might wish to avoid, but for communalists, this form of record provides a cultural foundation. Jesus frequently referred to the writings of the Old Testament, and we see in the defences of Peter, Stephen and Paul, as well as in Paul's preaching to the Jews, the significance of the nation's patriarchs and a constant referencing of God's wisdom given to the ancestors (for example, in Acts 3, 6, 7, 13).

While Westerners may seek genealogical databases in an endeavour to provide a feeling of grounding through discovering one's roots, this is fundamentally different from the way communal societies view their ancestors inhabiting the 'everywhen'. We may seek familial ties, but it is less likely that we would seek the moral advice an ancestor may have given or inquire regarding their philosophy. There is a Darwinian-based implicit assumption that we are apex dwellers who, because of this, have knowledge that is superior to that of all of our predecessors.

We have become accustomed to a temporal setting for our lives and our beliefs, but the defining of ourselves implicitly as players embedded in God's great drama[21] of Creation and human history requires a paradigm shift. Knowledge, or data, is retrieved now in milliseconds from the supposedly omniscient Internet, and, given our impatience, it may be difficult for us to imagine the deep learning intrinsic to village enculturation and the length of time this might take.

The educational importance of this implied depth of enculturation is seen in the many variants of the claim already mentioned: "Give me a child until he is seven and I will show you the man." Tom Wright described the methods that are used by communal groups in order to "fix important material in the communal memory", as including, "new and important stories are repeated over and over until the basic pattern of their telling is indelibly imprinted on the village mind."[22]

The birth to adulthood education of the next generation in communal and other contexts also involves the inculcation of values and mores as well as practical ways of living (food sources, for example), how interpersonal relationships are formed, and

---

[21] Bartholomew & Goheen, 2014
[22] Wright, 2015, p. 135

function, and all that is essential for physical, emotional, spiritual and relational growth and wellbeing. In doing this, it establishes and reinforces the worldview assumptions of normality for commune members. While there may be some similarities at times, the means by which this is accomplished through the teaching and learning methods used in communalism fundamentally differ from those in Western education systems. When Western countries colonised other countries and saw the tribal groups living in villages in what they deemed to be 'primitive' conditions, they decided that the people needed 'education'. (This was particularly true of mission societies, though their aim was inspired also by the need to teach the Gospel.) Tedla[23] raised a question regarding the missionaries' perception of a need for education, asking: What did they think we had been doing with our children for thousands of years? In the West, of course, the concept of education has been disassociated from the family or communal context, massified, commodified, and tasked with attempting to inculcate a State-determined culture for State purposes.

This family-to-State shift is not conducive to communal formation and maintenance. The significance of the individualism-inspired breaking down of communality in the education of children is highlighted by Irvine, speaking of the Māori culture in New Zealand. With reference to the aforementioned aphorism "It takes a village to raise a child", she wrote:

> Village life is a key element to Māori culture, so it's hard to know whether the reference was an off-the-cuff remark, or meant to carry a deeper meaning. But for modern parents everywhere, it strikes a chord. A gentle reminder: it takes a village to raise a child. And so often in modern life, new parents can find that village to be missing in action.[24]

A desire for this form of communal group has implications for non-village institutions, which are structures that, by their nature, are societal. In educational institutions, for example, individuals are brought together by government or parental decree to live as individuals who may or may not be relationally connected with many others but are called to work together to achieve stated purposes. This sociation is utilitarian and is intended to serve pragmatic purposes for individuals, for their families, and for the broader society. In educational institutions that take the name of Christ, given the human desire to relate and the biblical injunction to love each other, the development of a sense of commune is to be prioritised. This is despite the fact that in schools, we may include those who situate themselves within God's *covenant community* and those who do not. Naturally, such heterogeneity creates an environment that at times will not be conducive to shared meanings. While the theory

---

[23] Tedla, 1996
[24] Irvine, 2018, pare 2

of knowledge to which we hold may be seen as being fundamentally individualistic,[25] and one may create one's own meaning for language symbols, as mentioned, agreed-upon meaning is obviously essential for inter-individual communication.

> The majority of people . . . learn religion in communities—beginning with the community of the family. They learn it as the philosopher Ludwig Wittgenstein once brilliantly observed that language is learned: not by individuals independently making up their own tongues, but in a *community* of users sharing the same linguistic rules.[26]

We have alluded to the idea that we may be able to invent our own 'private language', but, obviously, we can only use spoken or written language as a communication medium if meaning has been developed and agreed upon with others. Powerful meaning-making and relational enculturation also require an embeddedness within a shared, coherent story, or metanarrative, that is generated and sustained by human interaction.

The establishment of a commune and the associated, powerful creation of shared meaning, while perceived as being for mutual benefit, is not without its costs, as with other forms of sociation. In a project in the Pacific Islands by Gegeo and Watson-Gegeo, they noticed that "both outsiders and school-educated Solomon Islanders cannot handle the rigorous way in which they [the indigenous people] subject ideas to intense questioning and other strategies of indigenous epistemology." [27] Defining truths as shared constructs is hard work. The metaphor used by the Kwara'ae people in Gegeo and Watson-Gegeo's project was a word meaning "pinching little by little along a thing" and referred to a form of,

> . . . systematic reasoning in laying out or evaluating a piece of evidence. The metaphor is drawn from gardening, where the end of a particular vine or root is located in a tangle of vines and roots by feeling along it carefully with the fingers. Metaphorically it refers to the epistemological strategy of locating truth or coming to a dependable conclusion by systematically reasoning through a tangle of evidence and possibilities.[28]

While commune members may not recognise that this is happening as it happens, it reflects an unconscious reality within tight-knit commune groups as they define reality and their existence in it together. Understanding perspectives on theology, the cosmos, reality, what it means to be, what it means to relate in a commune, and so on, is

---

[25] Miller, 2015
[26] Eberstadt, 2003, p. 212
[27] Gegeo & Watson-Gegeo, 2001, p. 78
[28] Ibid. p. 72

important for each individual in the group and for establishing the essence of the group's existence, internal dynamics, and any relationships outside the group.

This process inevitably also incurs a cost. In addition to group membership costs, such as financial commitments and, in religious settings in particular, physical and time costs related to particular religious observances, in a relational immersion into a group, there is, as always, the previously discussed identity cost: "Real understanding always has an identity cost."[29] Understanding between individuals requires each to undergo a blurring of understood self-definition; a fusion of two or more horizons of understanding, to use Gadamer's[30] terminology.

> In coming to see the other correctly, we inescapably alter our understanding of ourselves. Really taking in the other will involve an identity shift in us. That is why it is so often resisted and rejected. We have a deep identity investment in the distorted images we cherish of others.[31]

In the context of the relationship categories, the identity cost increases dramatically from individualism to communal relationships. As Westerners, we place further constraints on ourselves where potential communal involvement is concerned, and this restricts the relationship options within which we may feel *gezelligheid*. This is problematic in a Christian conversion sense, where the identity cost involved in profoundly changing identity and being incorporated into a different group (the Church) would be perceived to be very substantial. (c.f., 2 Corinthians 5:15: "And he died for all, that those who live should no longer live for themselves but for him who died for them and was raised again," and Galatians 2: 20: "I have been crucified with Christ, and I no longer live, but Christ lives in me.") The life we live in the Body of Christ, we live by faith in the Son of God, who loved us and gave himself for us. Of course, it is the work of the Holy Spirit to facilitate these changes, but for the non-Christian, in most cases, the perceived cost would outweigh perceived benefits. Otherwise, they would be Christians already.

Benedictine options?

As we consider the news from around the world and the real, perceived, or potential persecution that may befall us because we claim allegiance to Christ, it may be tempting to withdraw—go off the grids of social media, news, or even relationships with 'the World'. Withdrawing with pious intent from the World and its negative responses to the Gospel has a long history.

---

[29] Taylor, 2002, p. 141
[30] Gadamer, 2014
[31] Taylor, *op. cit.*, pp. 140–141

Originally, in fourth-century Egypt, many Christian monks (from *monachos* for a person who is one—i.e., single-minded or focused) chose to live alone. But soon Abba Pachomius (c. 292–346) organized more than five thousand of these monks into the Koinonia, a federation of small monastic cities where monks lived in communal houses of forty members, and shared buildings such as a church, refectory (dining hall), and infirmary for the sick. However, the ground plan and architecture of most medieval European monasteries, like Saint-Michel-de-Cuxa, were not inspired by Pachomius' cities, but by the monastic community Benedict of Nursia (c. 480–c. 547) founded at Monte Cassino, Italy, two hundred years later.[32]

Diedrich Bonhoeffer, writing regarding the cheapening of grace through the Christianisation of the world under the Roman Empire, wrote that: "This monasticism became a living protest against the secularisation of Christianity and the cheapening of grace."[33] Bonhoeffer's view and his Nazi Germany context led him, however, to the establishment of a form of monastic commune, the Finkenwalde Seminary, for training pastors who could lead an underground church during Germany's Nazi era. Two years after its establishment, however, the seminary was declared illegal and closed by the Gestapo. With a transition from the original meaning of monastery as a place for 'living alone', Dekar[34] noted that Bonhoeffer's intent was to eschew the traditional view of monasticism as being that of sequestered, celibate living. Rather than the abode of a hermit, the vision of Bonhoeffer was of a monasticism that provided a profound way for oblates 'to do life together'.

The withdrawal, or partial withdrawal of monks from society in general, in order to live communally with their God and each other, would appear to be antithetical to the missional mandate of Matthew 28:18–20 or Abraham Kuyper's encouragement for us to live lives in the world in order to work with Christ towards its redemption. Wilson-Hartgrove, however, likened the work of monastic communities to rhizomes beneath society that "spread beneath the surface, effecting change from below. It is a quiet revolution—one that is often ignored by the newspapers and usually missed by the historians. But, in the end, it is how God plans to save the world."[35] The historical importance of monastic orders was also outlined by Kaufman: "They eventually became involved in every aspect of human life. As a result, they changed the societies around them, as well as the cultures that transmit the fundamental values of any society."[36]

---

[32] Homik, 2010, p. 55
[33] Bonhoeffer, 1995, p. 46
[34] Dekar, 2008
[35] Wilson-Hartgrove, 2010, p. 18
[36] Kaufman, 2010, p. 31

They were the people who converted the pagan inhabitants of Europe to Christianity. They were the people who copied the Scriptures, and kept the learning of the past alive. They were the people who founded schools and hospitals. And they were the people who introduced the basic principles of democracy into society by electing their own leaders. They were the people who made manual labor respectable by including it in their daily lives. They were the people who taught us the meaning of time, by living disciplined lives governed by a schedule, and by inventing the clock that made such lives possible. Even the beginnings of the modern business corporation can be traced back to the medieval monasteries. Our whole way of life depends on things we now take for granted, things that were first introduced into society by the pre-Reformation monastic communities—especially the Benedictine monastic communities . . . . Perhaps the greatest contribution these communities have made is evangelism. Wherever and whenever we encounter evangelicals, from the first century to the twenty-first, we find them preaching. We first find them traveling throughout the Roman Empire preaching wherever people would listen to them. In the centuries following we find them preaching to the indigenous peoples of northern Europe, once again wherever and whenever they could gather a crowd. In the medieval era we find them preaching in the churches —until they are expelled from the pulpit, and then we find them preaching in the streets, in the marketplaces, in the fields and in homes, in jails and in taverns. After the Reformation we find them preaching to huge crowds in the open fields.[37]

Writing in more recent years, Bass commented on communal groups arising within an American evangelical context: "New Monasticism evolved as a response to the growing Constantinianism of American Christianity."[38] Scott Bessenecker has observed that the new monasticism is "partly a reaction to the self-absorbed life of material accumulation, career obsession and amusement fixation that is promoted in the West and that is now being exported around the world as a picture of 'the good life.'"[39] A number of other writers also have considered what might be described as a New Monasticism.[40]

At the margins of church and society, a "new monasticism" is emerging. This network of Christian communities seeks to enable its members to live out an authentic Christian life by loving each other and their neighbors. Believing that

---

[37] Ibid. p. 28
[38] Bass, 2018, para. 4
[39] Bessenecker, 2018, p. 187
[40] For example, Hart, 2006; Preston, 2005; Dekar, 2007; Dietterich, 2012; Dreher, 2018; Bass, 2004; Wilson-Hartgrove, 2008

Grayman-Simpson and Mattis listed what they termed the "essential dimensions" indicative of this new communal living. These were:

> (1) Anchoring of individual identity in group; (2) Transcendence of group duties and responsibilities over individual concerns; (3) Sanctity of social bonds and relations; (4) Primacy of social existence; and (5) Emphasis on sharing and contributing in support of the group.[42]

A list of "twelve Marks of New Monasticism", according to Nozaki was formulated in a "New Monasticism Gathering" where approximately sixty members from a number of different groups tried to agree on "a grassroots ecumenism and a prophetic witness within the North American church". The twelve points below contain references to relationships but also include rules relating to structure and governance.

1. Relocation to the abandoned places of Empire.

2. Sharing economic resources with fellow community members and the needy among us.

3. Humble submission to Christ's body, the church.

4. Geographical proximity to community members who share a common rule of life.

5. Hospitality to the stranger.

6. Nurturing common life among members of intentional community.

7. Peacemaking in the midst of violence and conflict resolution within communities along the lines of Matthew 18.

8. Lament for racial divisions within the church and our communities combined with the active pursuit of a just reconciliation.

9. Care for the plot of God's earth given to us along with support of our local economies.

10. Support for celibate singles alongside monogamous married couples and their children.

11. Intentional formation in the way of Christ and the rule of the community along the lines of the old novitiate [i.e., a probationary period that a novice undergoes before entering a religious order].

---

41 Dietterich, 2012, para. 3
42 Grayman-Simpson & Mattis, 2017, p. 128

12. Commitment to a disciplined contemplative life.[43]

A countercultural culture-within-a-culture example that has operated for millennia to provide a communal and deep enculturation of successive generations is seen in the communities of orthodox Jews around the world. Various endeavours in recent centuries have sought to establish communal practices that would lead to a holistic living context based on an Early Church model and to provide a biblically grounded, enculturation of the young. Significant groups that have formed have included those such as the Anabaptists and the modern Bruderhof Communities, Old Mennonites, and Amish, as well as denominational and non-denominational or ecumenical communities such as the Taizé monastic community in France. There have been many other groups, such as The Simple Way in Pennsylvania, and in Australia, a Baptist monastery that was established in the late 1990s, though it was not long-lasting. Paul Dekar quotes from a description of the Baptist monastery in Australia:

> Here some of the People of GOD from many Christian Communions live together as an intentional monastic community. In an age of growing fear and terrorism, we seek for peace and unity in a profound union with GOD. We have found it is the human heart that must first be disarmed. We strive to pray our life and to live our prayer, to be conscious, honest, simple and merciful towards all people and the earth. Here the "Prayer of the Heart"—of compassion and gratitude—has not failed. We share our life with any in need.[44]

These communes were established in order for members to separate themselves from a sinful culture by adopting an alternative, communal lifestyle. Some modern authors have claimed that, given the ills in our society, and particularly the intent of governments to enculturate children to their ideological position, such seeking may be valid. As Rod Dreher has written regarding communal living, but using community as a broader term:

> The fate of religion in America is inextricably tied to the fate of the family, and the fate of the family is tied to the fate of the community . . . . When both the family and the community become fragmented and fail, the transmission of religion to the next generation becomes far more difficult. All it takes is the failure of a single generation to hand down a tradition for the tradition to disappear from the life of a family and, in turn, of a community.[45]

Communalism, while an ideal that the Bible in a sense supports, may appear to be unworkable in our societies today and within the artificial organisational structures within which we work. While aspects of Dreher's *Benedictine Option*, and living,

---

[43] Nozaki, 2011, pp. 2–3
[44] Dekar, 2007, p. 382
[45] Dreher, 2017, p. 123

notionally or practically, apart from the mainstream society, may appeal, realistically, most situations in which we find ourselves must also conform to the dictates of external authorities such as secularist governments, and this introduces elements that can be destructive to genuine, Christ-centred, communal living. Just the same, Rod Dreher describes the necessity of seeking a *Benedict Option* as,

> The idea is that serious Christian Conservatives could no longer live business as usual lives in America, that we had to develop creative, communal solutions to help us hold onto our faith and our values in the world growing evermore hostile to them. We would have to choose to make a decisive lead into a truly countercultural way of living Christianity . . .[46]

In his Prologue to his third edition of *After Virtue: A Study in Moral Theory*, Alisdair MacIntyre wrote,

> Benedict's greatness lay in making possible quite a new kind of institution, that of the monastery of prayer, learning, and labor, in which and around which communities could not only survive, but flourish in a period of social and cultural darkness. The effects of Benedict's founding insights and of their instructional embodiment by those who learned from them were from the standpoint of his own age quite unpredictable. And it was my intention . . . to suggest that ours too is a time of waiting for new and unpredictable possibilities of renewal. It is a time for resisting as prudently and courageously and justly and temperately as possible the dominant social, economic, and political order of advanced modernity.[47]

We might note, however, that living in close proximity to other human beings and endeavouring to establish agreed-upon, socially permissible norms for the group is fraught with difficulties. One potentially negative outcome is the potential for the formation of an isolationist, inflexible fundamentalism and the total rejection of the beliefs and practices of others. (This was not the intention of many of the early Benedictines, who expressed their beliefs through their engagement with their broader communities.) In addition, there is the fickleness and changeability of fallen human beings concerned for their own interests, and the difficulties involved with finding a set of rules to which all will be committed wholeheartedly in the long term. Any such lack of rule ownership can provide a shaky foundation for communal living. Regarding the initial ideal of communal living, and writing concerning the establishment and maintenance of Bruderhof communal groups, Maendel quoted from a sermon by *Eberhard Arnold in 1926*, which spoke of the need for God's intervention:

---

[46] Dreher, 2017, p. 2
[47] MacIntyre, 2017, p. xvi

What drove us to this lifestyle, to this type of activity and community? [By 1920] the World War was over; the Revolution had run its course. We realized that this was an end, not a beginning. We longed to escape the tension, confusion, and deadly animosity. But we realized that we did not have the strength to live differently in a way that would answer our longing—to tread a path toward our goal of community and unity, of strength and joy, a path that in this degenerate creation would point to the new creation.

Then Jesus met us anew. Jesus met us in such perfect clarity that we had to accept the practical possibility of his lifestyle as it was given to us. We recognized the Sermon on the Mount, the parables of Jesus, and his words in sending out his disciples, as a character sketch of the people of the future and their way of community. We recognized it as a new planting of life from the Spirit . . . which like a tree, like light, like salt has to live according to its nature.[48]

Maendel also wrote that group members feel a deep sense of being "united with people of all centuries who have felt the demand of community that comes from the love of Christ", but that "love must be all-embracing or it is nothing."[49] However, three dangers were found to be inherent to the groups:

1. The danger of being "exclusive, isolated, narrow, both spiritually and practically"[50]

2. The second danger, which applies to all communal living, is one arising from *eros*, or mutual, particularly physical, attractions between members. This may deteriorate to an exclusive relationship that is confined to a love that may cut the individuals off from others.

3. The third danger of communal life is a lack of recognition of our imperfections, leading to judgment or taking offence at others' imperfections or weaknesses.

Practicalities

It seems, therefore, that the 'communal urge' is not primarily a historical legacy nor simply a response to immediate circumstances. Rather, it appears that within every (Western) society, just as there will be those who wish to be marginal, deviant, intensely individualistic or eccentric, so will there be those who seek comprehensive integration of the society as a whole, or of groups

---

[48] Maendel, 2019, paras. 2, 3
[49] Ibid., para 5
[50] Ibid., para 5

within it, groups which carry the society's 'true' meaning and purpose. No prompting is required for this trend: it is intrinsic to human society.[51]

MacIntyre conceded that not all communities, or communal groups, are benign or positive. Many can be oppressive and dangerous but the maintenance of Godly groups requires virtuous behaviours: and "the greatest of these is love" (1 Corinthians 13:13). He saw, however, a critical turning point in history was when the early Christians turned their allegiance away from the Roman Empire and towards a moral community where communal living allegiant to the Christ could survive the barbarism of the age. The stability of these groups' own intellectual and moral life was able to sustain them through the vicissitudes of the Dark Ages and beyond. A warning was added, however, by MacIntyre:

> And if the tradition of the virtues was able to survive the horrors of the last dark ages, we are not entirely without grounds for hope. This time [today] however the barbarians are not waiting beyond the frontiers; they have already been governing us for quite some time. And it is our lack of consciousness of this that constitutes our predicament. We are waiting not for a Godot, but for another—doubtless very different—St Benedict.[52]

Communal living, in the Benedictine sense, certainly has some appeal at times. It provides a 'safe place' for Christians, a place for meditation and prayer, a place for sharing and expressing Christ's love in a mutually accepting environment. The 'disarming of the heart' that is required in commune development pertains to relationships of all sorts, including not only human-to-human relationships but attitudes towards society's structures, hierarchies, economic activity, and so on. The education of successive generations, therefore, must be tightly controlled if the commune is to be sustained. It must be seen also in terms of long-term nurture and education by the family and the 'village', in much the same way that members of other village groups are educated.

> Essential to the persistence of Hutterite society in relatively unchanged form is of course the socialization system. The relation between the sexes, the age hierarchy, economic activity, attitudes to the outside world—all these depend on having members with a particular set of values and skills and certain perceptions of themselves, their society, their environment. The education system is geared up to having precisely such members, yet it is not simply the education system in its own right which achieves this. Like most aspects of Hutterite society the education system is integral to the wider life of the colony.

---

[51] Shenker, 1986, p. 2
[52] MacIntyre *op. cit.*, p. 263

92

Put otherwise, we may say that the very fact of living on the colony is in itself an education; the system of child-rearing is one element in the continuity of theory and practice and of specific colony practices. Just as much as education (in the formal sense) props up 'the system' so does 'the system' prop up education. A child growing up on a colony is meant to *learn* formally and to *experience* informally what it is to be a Hutterite. The two are meant to complement and reinforce one another, thus providing a system which is self-perpetuating because it is internally consistent. The aim of child-rearing is to make the child understand, accept and practice that consistency.[53]

Relationality is a key feature of communal living, but it must be noted that the development of the New Monastic movement was not solely for the purpose of relationship improvement. Some have formed out of a desire for deeper spirituality, others for altruistic reasons, and some, like The Simple Way, out of need and necessity. The idea of helping others, of sharing communally around meal tables and focusing together on Christ's Kingdom work may be alluring for Christians. Despite the exhortations through the New Testament to relate as members of the Body of Christ, as living stones in of a spiritual house, united as Christ's Bride, and so on, the establishment of such Christian communal living has proven difficult throughout post-Ascension history. There are several reasons for this.

First, there is the fallen nature that we have inherited along with its greed, desire for self-aggrandisement and self-promotion of individuals, and our desire for power and control. People may therefore wish to join communes for a range of reasons: a response to materialism, idealism, or romanticism, or out of selfish ambition.

Second, the individualism and organisation-driven societism of the West over centuries render the necessary and complete transformation of mindsets from individualism to communalism extremely difficult. Communal living may be established by a group at any time, but most are very short-lived. The transformation of an entire way of life is difficult for any human being to contemplate. For that reason, and in order to facilitate the difficult process, Shenker suggested the following conditions must be met if one is to form what he terms an "intentional community":

(1) It was founded as a conscious and purposive act;

(2) Membership is voluntary and based on a conscious act (even if the member was born in the community);

(3) The group sees itself as separate from and different from its environment and relates as a group to (or withdraws as a group from) its environment;

---

[53] Shenker, 1986, p. 89

(4) The community is relatively self-contained—most members can potentially live their entire lives in it (or for the period during which they are members);

(5) Sharing is part of the community's ideology;

(6) The community has collective goals and needs and expects members to work towards their satisfaction;

(7) The ideology claims that the goals of the community, even if orientated to the benefit of the individual, can only be obtained in a collective framework;

(8) Ultimately the community, or people appointed by the community, but not the individual, is the source of authority;

(9) The general way of life of the community is considered to be inherently good, i.e. is an end in itself over and above its instrumental value;

(10) The community's existence has a moral value and purpose which transcend the timespan of individual membership.[54]

Third, the transformation takes time for a new normal, with new norms, new values, new assumptions, and new practices, to be enculturated. The communal living cultures that have persisted over long periods of time, such as the 30,000-strong members of the two hundred and thirty Hutterite groups, have grown over the last four hundred and fifty years. Lasting communal integrity implies that their communal living has been tightly structured, with close adherence to the beliefs and practices that are passed down from generation to generation. A reason for the communal longevity of Christian groups compared with secular counterparts is indicated in research by Sosis: "Preliminary results from survivorship analysis support this hypothesis; religious communes are more likely than secular communes to survive at every stage of their life course . . . . Secular communes are simply not as successful as religious communes at maintaining their ideological belief among members."[55] This, Sosis claimed, was because, not unexpectedly, "groups that strongly believe in the ideology that unites them will be better able to overcome obstacles and tragedies that may result in the dissolution of less 'devout' groups."[56] Truly communalist groups tend to lack the sacred-secular divide found in individualistic cultures. Instead, they are pervaded by holistic religious ideas and ones that insist that the members' lives reflect the sacred and socially permissible norms of the group.[57] Taylor pointed to the fact that religious life in ancient, or tribal, situations was "inseparable from social life"[58] and that the New

---

[54] Shenker, 1986, p. 7
[55] Sosis, 2000, pp. 70, 76
[56] Ibid., p. 80
[57] Moemeka, 1998
[58] Taylor, 2007, p. 147

Testament supported this idea with many examples of solidarity in families, tribes, and so on, in their Kingdom living.

Of course, there are forces that may work against the establishment and maintenance of a commune, as Bonhoeffer found as his was dismantled by the Gestapo. Other groups, even genuinely Christian groups, may be considered a cult or in some way dangerous to society and be vilified in the media and 'legal' means sought to eradicate them. Perhaps it is the case, therefore, that for these reasons the commitment to loyalty within religious groups is stronger than for non-religious groups.

Commencing a communal group from scratch is difficult. For Benedictine communities, the *Rule* becomes of great importance as a plumb line against which the practice of the commune is measured. For communal living to last, it is essential that a degree of stasis is guaranteed. New members coming into the commune must enter on the commune's terms and must not be permitted to bring change other than that conferred by their membership as individuals. Where individualism is permitted to play a significant role, a breakdown of communality will become inevitable. Another significant problem in Christian groups today is a lack of agreed-upon definitions and doctrines: What is a Christian? What does a Christian believe? How does a Christian behave? What does a Christian do? (These are questions that have become impossible for the World to answer due to the plethora of widely differing responses that Christians might give.) In this context, the concept of a communally structured group, where meanings were clearly and deeply shared, with deep acculturation into beliefs and practices (and deeper than Benedict's *Rule of Life*), may certainly hold some attraction.

Members of a commune are therefore more likely, though not exclusively, to have a common purpose that has been negotiated in some way and that finds acceptance across the group. Anyone who does not concur may leave the group and seek a group with a purpose more to their liking. **A fundamental difference here between 'community' and 'commune' is that, while those in the latter may share a teleology or purpose, they also share an ontology—a sense of being—and in this case, the sense that 'to be' a human being is 'to be in communion' with others. This is a fundamental distinction that separates communality from each of the other frames of relationality in the series.**

8. Communalism in Cultural and Biblical Contexts

> The Yolngu [Norther Australian Aboriginal] child is integrated from infancy into an extensive social network where everyone is explicitly identified first and foremost according to relationship. This is constantly and consciously reinforced in all social interaction. Living in a story telling culture, the Yolngu child begins a comprehensive cultural education at an early age. These stories are no fairy tales, myths or legends. Each story, whether about creation events, the spirit world or a moral lesson, is told as truth. The relationships to the child listener of the characters, country, clans and animals which feature in the stories, are made explicit . . . as the story unfolds. Thus the identity of the child with the Yolngu world is built.[1]

At the conclusion of the previous chapter, the point was made that a fundamental difference exists between our use of the terms 'community' and 'commune'. The difference is that, while those in the latter may share a purpose, they also share an ontology—a sense of being. In this chapter, which examines the case of village communalism, we see illustrations of what it might mean 'to be' a human being in the sense of 'being in communion' with others. For example, in terms of a 'sense of being', an African culture based on *ubuntu*—I am because we are—has a different 'sense of being' from a Western, individualistic culture that has a sense of I am because I am. In the previous chapter, we saw examples of communal living in subcultures, primarily within Western contexts. We normally find that in order to understand a culture, it is helpful to compare it with another culture, and most commonly, we compare it with our own. Other cultures, in this way, can act as a kind of 'find the differences' puzzle by which we see our culture and our cultural perspectives. Only by doing this can we see clearly many of the differences and the assumed 'normal' that we have in us that has been embedded in us by our culture, and then reflect on the differences. This also gives us ideas, or hints, as to how Christian communion may function in our own group settings.

---

[1] Cooke, 1990, p. 43

There are many examples of culture comparisons in Scripture, and many of the players in God's recorded drama showed they understood their culture compared with others, and also their ability to understand others. One example we might take is seen in the ministry of the Apostle Paul, who demonstrated his understanding of cultural differences in the way he taught his Jewish compatriots and those in the Greek culture. To the Jews, Paul told the story of their people, referencing and using illustrations from their Scriptures. By contrast, perhaps one of the clearest cross-cultural examples is his discourse on the Areopagus in Acts 17:22–31. He spoke their language and provided local context with his references to the legend of Epimenides and the sacrifice of sheep to the various gods across Athens. This included Epimenides' injunction that where areas did not have a designated deity, an altar was to be constructed and a sacrifice was to be made to the 'unknown god'. He also quoted from Epimenides and the Greek poet Aratus. The teaching style he adopted was the oratorical, debating format with which his hearers were familiar, and for which they came to the Areopagus. These two cultures that Paul addressed had different understandings of what it means 'to be', what 'truth' is and how it is discovered, and how truth is communicated. They had different senses of what was 'normal'.

In this chapter, then, we will move from looking at contrasting subcultures to looking at examples of communal life in non-Western settings in Africa and South America. The long-established communal living that is foundational to tribal and village cultures differs from the rather ephemeral, neo-monastic communal groups established in recent years in Western societies. There are, however, features that stand out more starkly for us due to their contrasted distinctiveness. These may be seen by briefly trying to see life through the eyes of those whose worldview assumptions, beliefs, and actions are embedded in and flow from a communal sense of being.

African contexts

> Communalism is seen as central to the Afrocultural social ethos.[2]
> A crucial distinction thus exists between the African view of man and the view of man found in Western thought: in the African view it is the community which defines the person as a person, not some isolated static quality of rationality, will or memory.[3]

Fundamental to developing cultures, communalism is a system that gives primacy to the group; organisation is hierarchical, life is sacrosanct, and a holistic religion is a way of life.[4] Each member is seen as a part of the whole, having been born into the

---

[2] Mbiti, 1970, p. 409
[3] Menkiti, 1979, p. 158
[4] Moemeka, 1998

group and raised as a group member through an education and enculturation process lasting up to thirty years. Actions of mature group members are seen as being significant only if they are relevant to the whole group. A significant, though obvious, point regarding such communal groups is that one is *born* into it and does not choose to be a member: "Such a community is not created as a result of the coming together of individuals. It is an evolved community whose membership is hereditary."[5] This is an important distinction for Christians. In terms of the Church, or the communion of the saints, this is something into which one must be *born again,* with the hereditary aspect coming through sonship with Christ.

In traditional African tribal village contexts, the individual is "defined by reference to the environing community"[6], but it goes much further than that in that the embeddedness of the individual is also in the physical environment and strongly linked to ancestral spirits. For our purposes here, however, we will not be too concerned with the relationships with the physical environment and the spirits, but with the interpersonal relationships within the commune and traditional village life. These relationships are in stark contrast to the individualism of the West and other items in the relationship category series. The communal structure in African village settings cannot be overemphasised and forms the "very fabric of traditional African life."[7] According to Nyasani, the reasons for the development of close-knit communalism in Africa included the harsh living conditions, such as the physical environment, marauding wild animals, and the threat of intertribal conflict.[8] These drove people to develop a particular form of supportive, interpersonal relationship in order to survive. While the influence of the colonising West has been substantial throughout much of the African continent, there are many African academics and researchers who are studying traditional ways and their value.

Perhaps the most common expression of holistic relationality in African settings has been the Nguni term *ubuntu,* which we have mentioned already, a term that is heard in the West due to its use by Desmond Tutu. *Ubuntu* is most commonly referred to in English as "I am because we are", and across Africa, there are many similar words that are used in different languages, for example, *bumuntu, gimuntu, umundu, umuntu,* and so on.[9] According to Kauka, the word is made up of '*U*', the Bantu equivalent of 'the', '*Bu*', the state of being, and '*Ntu*', 'human', hence 'the state of being human'.[10] It is a statement, however, that implies a level of unity at the extreme end, in human terms,

---

[5] Ibid., p. 124
[6] Ibid., p. 171
[7] Higgs, 2010, p. 2416
[8] Nyasani, 1989
[9] Nyathu, 2004
[10] Kauka, 2018

from individualism. In it, the *I* dissolves into the *we*. Descartes's '*cogito ergo sum*' (I think therefore I am), is often quoted in Western contexts and Kauka uses the expression to demonstrate that in the West, *reason* is definitive of being human, whereas in African cultures, it is the *we* that is definitive.[11] This is not to say that the individual or the self are not recognised or important in these cultures. While for these communalists, the sense of belonging to a unified commune or tribe operates at the level of intuition or assumption, the individual still engages with the world through their senses and reasoning as applied to their physically distinct, individual, physical bodies and contexts. An example regarding personal needs is given in the following: "When one's neighbor is eating all kinds of harmful insects, one should hasten to warn such a neighbor, otherwise when she/he falls sick with cough or other ailments, her/his cough or noises of agony at night will disturb one's sleep."[12] The emphasis in communalism is not on the negation of the individual but, rather, the perspective that each individual should not, in some way, take precedence over the group.

Finding an English expression equivalent of *ubuntu* is fraught, however, and the problem is not made any easier for individualists who may look at communal groups and say, but there is no *we* without *I*-s. Mnyaka and Motlhabi described the difficulty also in terms of our understanding of time.[13] We seem to understand what the passing of time is, but actually defining time itself is another thing altogether. Bishop Desmond Tutu, who was the person to make the term famous in the West, also noted that *ubuntu* is very difficult to translate, but gave the following explanation:

> *Ubuntu* is very difficult to render into a Western language. It speaks of the very essence of being human. When we want to give high praise to someone we say, "*Yu, u nobuntu*"; "Hey, so-and-so has *ubuntu*." Then you are generous, you are hospitable, you are friendly and caring and compassionate. You share what you have. It is to say, "My humanity is caught up, is inextricably bound up, in yours." We belong in a bundle of life. We say ,"A person is a person through other persons." It is not, "I think therefore I am." It is rather: "I am human because I belong. I participate, I share." A person with *ubuntu* is open and available to others, affirming others, does not feel threatened that others are able and good, for he or she belongs in a greater whole and is diminished when others are humiliated or diminished, when others are tortured or oppressed, or treated as if they were less than who they are.[14]

---

[11] It is hard to imagine how the concept of solipsism could even exist in communal cultures.
[12] Avoseh, 2012, p. 246
[13] Mnyaka & Motlhabi, 2005
[14] Tutu, 1999, p. 31

Nyathu saw *ubuntu*'s importance as a value system in the way that it has "been the backbone of many African societies"[15] and the source of actions and attitudes. The word implies a deep, and particular, sense of being (ontology), a way of knowing, discerning truth and understanding (epistemology), and a value system (axiology)—giving "existential authenticity"[16] to African viewpoints. This philosophy of life is not restricted to traditional villages, however, and even flows on to government levels with the South African Government, for example, publishing the following statement:

> The principle of caring for each other's well-being will be promoted, and a spirit of mutual support fostered. Each individual's humanity is ideally expressed through his or her relationship with others and theirs in turn through a recognition of the individual's humanity. *Ubuntu* means that people are people through other people. It also acknowledges both the rights and the responsibilities of every citizen in promoting individual and societal well-being.[17]

The idea of such a deep interrelatedness functioning in village settings, or even at a state level, involves such different and deeply held sets of values, beliefs, and practices, "recognizing the humanity of others in its infinite variety of content and form."[18] This is difficult for individualistic Westerners to fully grasp. What remains particularly difficult for us is the idea of loss of identity in the 'other'. Humanity expressed towards others, charity and love, sympathy, and a sense of belonging we readily experience, but we have difficulty with the 'I am because we are' that defines the self in the group and without the group, identity is lost completely. The outworking of this *ubuntu* philosophy, or perspective in reality, is to be towards communal living, sharing (as opposed to competition), harmony, hospitality, respect and responsiveness one for the other and therefore has an obvious practical connection with biblical principles.[19]

Problems

Perhaps it is tempting to regard living in a relational framework founded on *ubuntu* as being a human ideal, and certainly it appears to be biblical. Within a South African context, however, Blankenberg and Malukeke[20] saw problems relating to the practice of *ubuntu* due to a lack of a clear and comprehensive definition for the term and potential *ubuntu* practices, and note that it is often used inappropriately outside its cultural context. Waghid and Smeyers concluded that *ubuntu*, as it is presented, needs

---

[15] Nyathu, 2004, p. 3
[16] Kauka, 2018, p. 43
[17] South African Government, 1997, p. 12
[18] Van der Merwe, 1996, p. 76
[19] Hailey, 2008
[20] Blankenberg, 1999; Malukeke, 1999

to evolve with the changing conditions in society, saying that "as an ideology it relies too much on the extraordinary: luck, miracles, and an ambiguous concept of natural goodness. *Ubuntu* is not enough because it fails to supplement . . . its innate optimism about the natural goodness of humankind with what I call the ordinary."[21] As seen with the example of the Hutus and Tutsis that was mentioned in the chapter on collectivism, the fallen nature of sinful human beings is certainly a factor that requires consideration. Hailey expanded on this using the term, community:

> It is important not to overlook the negative consequences of [the] synergistic relationship between an individual and the community, and in turn how easy it is for community tensions to lead to violence. Communities with a strong, cohesive identity may result in individual members of a particular community or ethnic group supporting and sympathizing with those that espouse evil acts. This is a grim reminder of the negative consequences of community cohesion, and how easy it is for different communities to be mobilized by evil acts. In recent years this dark side of African civil society has played itself out across Africa—in Rwanda, the Congo, Liberia, Northern Uganda, Sierra Leone, the Sudan, and Zimbabwe. It is a sad fact of life that all too often these events are rarely reported in the West. It is only recently that we have any real knowledge of the millions who have died as a consequence of communal conflict in the Congo.[22]

Caring

The fallenness of humanity to one side, however, an illustration of the caring aspect of *ubuntu* is the story, perhaps apocryphal, of the anthropologist who placed a basket of fruit at the foot of a tree near an African village and told the children that he would start a race and the first to reach the tree could have the fruit. The story goes that children joined hands and arrived at the tree together, sharing the fruit equally. When asked why they did this, the reply was given as, "*Ubuntu*. How can one of us be happy if all the others are sad?"

The lived network of relationships, in communalist cultures, means in biblical terms that when one suffers all suffer and if one is honoured, all are honoured (1 Corinthians 12:26). Ruch and Anyaanwu made the point that in that cultural context, the honouring of success and the sharing of glory by the whole group is, "not only psychologically (as one would rejoice when one's local soccer team has won a match) but ontologically: each member of the group is really part of the honor."[23] Each group member becomes

---

[21] Waghid & Smeyers, 2012, p. 17
[22] Hailey, 2008, p. 9
[23] Venter, 2004, p. 143

102

his or her neighbour's keeper and thus, the welfare of the group is sustained. The communal spirit ensures that "the hungry be fed, that the sick be looked after, the community takes care of what the individual does for a living during periods of illness, that orphans be fostered without delay."[24]

Moemeka listed five fundamental principles for communal living: Supremacy of the communal groups, Sanctity of authority, Usefulness of the individual, Respect for the elderly, and Religion as a way of life. "In communalistic communities, leaders are not just citizens of the community. They are both the temporal and spiritual heads . . . . all communalistic societies strongly believe in the fluid type of leadership structure emanating from the philosophy of gerontocracy [i.e., leadership by elders]."[25] The ideal of *ubuntu* relationships is the promotion of humble thoughtfulness and consideration of others, and therefore being generous and hospitable. The 'I am because we are' implies a particular moral stance vis-à-vis others in the group, but not only for altruistic reasons, but because each group member's identity is tied to the others. Just the same, the moral imperatives become group ones rather than purely individual ones.

> In a communalistic social order, community welfare undergirds actions. Nothing done, no matter how important and useful it is to the individual, is considered good unless it has relevance for the community. No misfortune, no matter how distinctly personal, is left for the individual to bear all alone. The community laughs together and also cries together.[26]

South America

As mentioned, African cultures are not the only ones to function in communalist ways. There are similarities between the African, Asian, Hispanic and Middle Eastern/Arabic cultures, but there are also distinctions. Some may be more individualistic, others more collectivist. As Westerners, we tend to overlay our concern for the individual over our understanding of collectivist or communalist cultures, and sometimes we also confuse collectivism with communalism.

In South America, we find that three relational categories are particularly visible. First, due to the media-based colonisation of the continent through movies, television shows and social media, in the cities, individualism is rising as each generation makes more use of technology. Second, in the city, there has been, and continues to be, a strong sense of collectivism. The origin of collectivism in Hispanic South America appears to be its importation from Spain with the post-Columbus conquests of the continent, and Spain had been heavily influenced by the North African Moors who had

---

[24] Moemeka, 1998, p. 130
[25] Ibid., p. 129
[26] Ibid., p. 124

lived in Spain for nearly eight centuries. (Today there still exist many words in Spanish that have Moorish roots—for example, *ojalá* (hopefully) from the Arabic, *InshAllah*—'if God wills'.)

The third relational framework is found in the village cultures and is a form of communalism. In this instance, the village groups to which we will refer specifically are those in Bolivia—where the author spent many years. People living in these villages do so under similar circumstances to those outlined for African villages above. In the villages, communal relationship structures have been established and maintained over millennia as people have been constrained to live together long-term in close proximity. Oviawe refers to the Latin American Spanish word *convivencia*, literally meaning 'living together' as the Spanish equivalent to the African *ubuntu*:

> Comparing and contrasting *ubuntu* with *convivencia*, Luschei posits that the attributes of *convivencia*—consisting of "active respect for others, solidarity, fair play and equity"—are in strong alignment with how Desmond Tutu envisions a person who practices the *ubuntu* ethos as being "open and available to others, affirming of others . . . not . . . threatened that others are able and good" . . . . Although *ubuntu* and *convivencia* are localized and situated within the unique contexts of their respective societies, they share a common message of collectivism and humanness.[27]

As with African contexts, the relational framework in the villages is holistic—involving not only interpersonal relationships but very deep-seated relationships, or perceived relationships, with ancestors, spirits, and elements within the environment. In Western objectivism, elements in the environment are observed objectively, but in these village contexts, the environment expresses itself to the human. While the Quechua and Aymara people of Bolivia and other parts of South America have numerous deities, one of the most important ones is *Pachamama*—Big Mother or Mother Earth.[28] Beliefs concerning spirits inhabiting rocks, trees, rivers, and mountains are also common. The personal relationships, combined with the other perceived relationships, yield a sense of embeddedness within a metaphysical universe, as opposed to a Western individualist's objectivist view. This view has been largely maintained despite four centuries of Hispanic governance and the recent Western influences through the introduction of communication technologies.

Interpersonal relationships within the village are strong, and village members are seen as part of the extended family, where everyone may be referred to as an uncle or aunt. Socialisation begins from birth and may include village members giving a newborn a gift and, in return, taking a small clipping of hair to indicate acceptance into the group.

---

[27] Oviawe, 2016, p. 8
[28] C.f., the references heard at times in the West to "Mother Nature".

104

As in the collectivism in the Hispanic cities, group member bonding also includes people considered as 'godparents' (*padrinos*), or adopted 'symbolic relatives' (*parientes simbólicos*). These also provide a relational context through *quid pro quo* arrangements of responsibilities. Trusting, *quid pro quo* arrangements also extend beyond relatives and fictive relatives to the group as a whole, and mention has been made of the *ayne* system of shared work. (This sense of cooperative working together is also reflected in the African concept of '*shosholoza*'.) Where larger projects are required, that is, requiring more than a single village, *mancomunidades* [associations which may involve a number of villages] are formed to coordinate the effort. This is possible due to the common ancestry and language of the villages in the region.

Some other features of the village communal living that may be contrasted with Western individualism or collectivism include the following, and in them, we also see an underlying fragility of this form of communal living. The ideals and the practices may exist, but in the sinful human heart lie the seeds of both love and animosity:

- When visiting another person, no announcement or arrangement for the visit is required—one simply arrives.

- Others are trusted and taken at their word. Obviously, as fallen human beings, there are cases where this does not happen, but it is a general rule.

- All members of the village are referred to using the informal personal pronoun (*tu*) if the speaker is using Spanish. It is "*tu a tu*" (you to you)—everyone is on the same level socially, and confrontation is minimised.

- There are Quechua terms for please and a formal thank you (*allichu* and *anchata agradisiyki*—which has Spanish roots), but these seem to be so rarely used that some think they do not exist. The reason for this is the oneness of relationships.

- Contentment is seen in a social context—of living together in harmony, where, as much as possible, there is a unity regarding opinions, and the availability of mutual assistance when needed.

- The closely bonded relationships within the village are strongly guarded, and potential damage is to be avoided as much as possible. An example of this is seen when a great deal of effort is expended to find the father if an unattached girl in the village becomes pregnant. Because everyone in the village is 'related' in one way or another to all the others, any doubt concerning paternity can cause mistrust and suspicions and therefore harm relationships.

- Greetings, as in African village contexts, specify relational intensity. While village members are seen as being equal as human beings, greetings in Quechua reflect a depth of friendship or endearment. A father, for example, may be referred to as *papa,* or *papito,* or *papitay*, with increasing depth of affectivity.

-        An interesting feature of the maintenance of good relationships that we do not encounter in the West is the fear that through witchcraft or in the afterlife, another may seek vengeance. It is especially advisable therefore to stay in a good relationship with someone who is dying so that they may not bring harm to you from the spirit world.

-        The relationality that forms the foundation for village communal existence is also supported by three underlying laws that are instilled in communal members from a young age: Do not lie, do not be lazy, and do not steal. Each of these refers directly to the maintenance of good relationships, and the breaking of any or all of them would not only harm or break relationships but would also disrupt the efficiency of the village.

-        Religion and holistic, metaphysical relationality are inexorably linked. Everything in the environment has a sacred quality. Where other religious ideas are introduced from other cultures, some degree, often substantial, of syncretism will be adopted.

-        As mentioned previously, the intimate, being-a-part-of relationship with Creation has been described as 'dividuation'—being a 'dividual' as opposed to being an *in*dividual.

It is also interesting to note that communalists seem to have a different approach to the passing of time compared with individuals or societies. African groups exist, obviously, in the present, but again, there is a sense that existence is inextricably bound to the past, though there is a belief in the presence of ancestral spirits and the wisdom that is passed down through successive generations. In Aymara communal villages, when asked to point to the future, they indicate behind themselves. They face the past. For many in communal groupings, without the structures of a modern, Western 'society', importance is placed more on events rather than time. We may find that some event, such as a church service, may start an hour or more late, an invitation to a home for dinner at 8 pm, may mean dinner will be served perhaps at 10 pm. And within a Christian context, we are also called to view time differently. God is not someone who is restricted by our understanding of time. Within the context of the Church in communion, there exists, or should exist, a sense being embedded in both the flow of time in God's story through all of history so far, and in the New Heaven and Earth future.

Further biblical links

No doubt, as you have read the preceding material in this book, you will have thought of biblical references or examples. God-human, human-human, God-Creation, and human-Creation relationships form the fundamental structure for the entire Creation, so we might expect to see references throughout Scripture . . . and we do. In this brief section, we consider some implications from a few examples from Jesus' time on earth and the century following.

The first thing we see as we look at the life of Christ is the village context into which he was born. Due to the close physical proximity and family ties, as well as the setting apart of God's people as a larger group, elements of collective and communal living could be assumed. As a young boy, we see Jesus talking to the religious leaders in the temple while His parents began to make their way home to Nazareth with their relatives and friends, presuming that Jesus was a part of the close group travelling together. During Jesus' ministry, of course, we see Him living in a very close relationship with His disciples for three years. In some senses, there were communal aspects of their relationship, but at times the small group acted as a collective ingroup, with Jesus at the centre. At least James and John considered the destruction of those who might be defined as outgroups (Luke 9:54).

Jesus and His disciples lived together, ate together, and travelled together, as the followers were discipled to be like their Master. We might note, however, that in Jesus' teaching, we see someone who did not teach by having the group members share till they came to a consensus. He was the source of knowledge, and He made the decisions. At least in the pieces of His teaching that we have in the New Testament, we also see Him using stories and parables, metaphors and illustrations, leaving the teaching very incomplete in a sense. He knew, of course, that the Holy Spirit would continue to teach and lead God's people into all truth (John 16:13) for the following millennia as His people connected with the Father individually and corporately, receiving revealed truth as individuals, or sharing revealed meaning in societies, communities, collectives, and communes.

Following Jesus' ascension, the disciples in the early Church are often seen by us to be living in an example of communalism. When we think of this, however, we usually illustrate it with the account of the members holding everything in common (Acts 2:44). Perhaps this is our tendency as individuals to be concerned with our ownership of our things and as we read the account in Acts, we naturally interpret it in terms we understand as individualists living with some connection to groups of Christian brothers and sisters. In the context of the Acts 2:44 statement from Peter's sermon on the Day of Pentecost, however, we see more detail of their communing together:

> Peter replied, "Repent and be baptized, every one of you, in the name of Jesus Christ for the forgiveness of your sins. And you will receive the gift of the Holy Spirit. The promise is for you and your children and for all who are far off—for all whom the Lord our God will call." With many other words he warned them; and he pleaded with them, "Save yourselves from this corrupt generation." Those who accepted his message were baptized, and about three thousand were added to their number that day. They devoted themselves to the

apostles' teaching and to the fellowship, to the breaking of bread and to prayer. Everyone was filled with awe, and many wonders and miraculous signs were done by the apostles. All the believers were together and had everything in common. Selling their possessions and goods, they gave to anyone as he had need. Every day they continued to meet together in the temple courts. They broke bread in their homes and ate together with glad and sincere hearts, praising God and enjoying the favor of all the people. And the Lord added to their number daily those who were being saved. (Acts 2:38–47)

The imagery here is not one of a group of friends as individuals sitting around singing Kum Ba Ya! Nor is it a structured society. And it seems to go beyond a loose-knit community of individuals, as many modern church congregations may seem to be. This group appears to function as communal living, but not in the modern sense of commune or monasticism, as the Church members probably still lived separately in homes scattered through the city. Some of the things we may note include:

- Peter's message was one of repentance and baptism, of turning from a works-based religion to allegiance to the Saviour. This radical heart transformation, evidenced in action, was a unifying factor that provided, and continues to provide, a unifying bonding for God's people.

- The gift of the Holy Spirit was given, thereby providing to all believers the stamp of God's ownership as sons and daughters in the family of the Most High.

- God's calling to His people implies a kinship connection between Church members.

- The new disciples "devoted themselves". There was a strong, forsaking-all-else, type of alignment of the wills of the commune members.

- They focused on the teaching of the apostles and thereby developed meaning together under the teaching of the apostles and the ministrations of the Holy Spirit. We do not have recorded all of the teaching content of the Apostles, but from other references, and given the fact that the new disciples in Jerusalem were local or expatriate Jews, the coherent narrative within which the meaning would have been embedded would have flowed from the history of God's dealings with His chosen people.

- They broke bread together. There is something about eating a meal together that brings humans together. This is something that business people understand well and practice with the proverbial business lunch. The sharing of food and drink creates a bond, and the technical term is commensalism—to share a meal around a table (Latin, *mensa*). The first instance we see in Scripture was a shared piece of fruit in the Garden, and there are many instances of food hospitality through the biblical narrative. Not inconsequentially, we see Jesus sharing food with His disciples and at the Last Supper initiating a commensalism dedicated to remembering Him and his sacrifice—a bonding practice we continue to this day.

- They prayed together. God's people seeking His face together in prayer is a significant practice that distinguishes us from those around us in the World.

- They 'were' together. Perhaps similar to the 'we are' idea of *ubuntu*, as they met corporately with the implied close physical proximity, there was a unified sense of 'being'.

- They had everything in common, pooling resources and proceeds from selling possessions so that nobody would be in need. This exemplified an *agape*, giving, love for each other, a love that overcame not only greed but even the human tendency to claim of something, 'this is mine!'.

- They met daily: A repeated corporate practice together. As disruptive as this must have been to their previous normal living, there was a determination to commune together.

- With gladness and sincerity, they praised God together—another continuing communal practice with a unified and unifying focus.

- While the second part of the quote above focuses on 'doing' things together, the essence from the first half is the idea of 'being', being made new with any 'doing' flowed from a new sense of 'being'—a new creation: the Body, the Church, the Bride.

We might add a note here regarding hospitality. As David Smith has pointed out, the depiction of the separation of sheep and goats in Matthew 25 is on the basis of a number of criteria, one of which is the treatment of the stranger, the alien, the foreigner.[29] As mentioned, this level of hospitality, of welcoming in the stranger, is probably not a common practice in the West but was, and is, in Middle Eastern cultures. By way of illustration, two young Australians who were visiting the Middle East as tourists a few years ago were invited home for a meal by a very friendly and hospitable family. The head of the family turned out to be what they presumed to be a Taliban leader, and at the end of the meal, gave the Australians clear instructions regarding which parts of the city would be dangerous to visit the next day. Such protection of a foreigner who is a guest is something we find taught and practised throughout the Old Testament.

One of the features of this level of hospitality is that it is not only strangers, or foreigners, but *enemies*, who are welcomed to share a meal. Apart from the custom of hospitality, an invitation to an enemy would indicate that the host feels, or is wishing to

---

[29] David Smith, 2009

be seen as feeling, that he or she is strong enough not to be afraid of the foe. We see examples of this in the Bible, but perhaps the most striking and familiar example for us is the invitation of Jesus to Judas to share his last meal before the crucifixion. Then, there is the current invitation of our Lord to join with Him in a meal as we celebrate Holy Communion—an invitation to us, who were His enemies (Romans 5:10), to share a remembrance meal with Him.

Other communal facets are seen in the New Testament in the accounts of the life, teaching, and ministry of the Apostle Paul. These include his close living with at least some of those whom he was discipling, and we also see a communal sense within the Church at large, with the collection Paul took back to the Jerusalem congregation. In His teaching, he referred very frequently to the 'wisdom of the ancestors', as it were, as he, like Stephen and the other New Testament writers, recounted the stories and history of God's dealings with His people. One feature of the new covenantal relationship God had with His Church was that there was not only one person, as there had been with Jesus, who carried the message and who taught. All of the disciples were told to disperse with the Gospel and to disciple others to do likewise. There seemed to be the sense that it was God's message, revealed by God, to multiple individuals, even though there was always the problem of some individuals confusing the message deliberately or unintentionally. Though various people received the Gospel message in order to spread it, the communion-forming factor in the process was God's intervention so that Paul could say, "What, after all, is Apollos? And what is Paul? Only servants, through whom you came to believe—as the Lord has assigned to each his task. I planted the seed, Apollos watered it, but God made it grow" (1 Corinthians 3:5–6). This constant, revelatory intervention by God is a critical factor. In many human communes, there can be a tendency for knowledge to stagnate as limited knowledge (and ignorance!) is shared repeatedly. God's intention is that the communion of His Church should grow, and that corporate process will take us eventually into Eternity.

> Because the Spirit is a gift, not to individuals but to a people gathered by God into a community of faith, the interpretation of Scripture under the guidance of God's Spirit is not primarily the task of individual scholars undertaken in the privacy of their own studies. First and foremost, it is the task of the church in public acts of witness and worship. Biblical scholarship is properly done when it is put in service of that task.[30]

Human growth and development, deepening relationships, progress, and the acquiring of knowledge, are not to be for the benefit of the individual, though that may be a side effect. Neither is it for the benefit of the core of an ingroup, nor simply for the

---

[30] Murray Rae, 2003, pp. 295–296

structure of a society, or simply for a better connectedness in a community. Instead they are to be seen as being for God's Kingdom purposes. Not mine, not my group's, but for His Bride, the Church growing, "until we all reach unity in the faith and in the knowledge of the Son of God and become mature, attaining to the whole measure of the fullness of Christ."[31]

Creating commune?

The call to the Communion of the Saints, of which Bonhoeffer[32] wrote, does not only apply to a monastic style of living, though it may. So, if we see a need, how might we develop communality as believers in the individualistic West? As we have seen, there are many reasons why people congregate in communal relationships that are deeper than those in most of the other categories we have considered. There may be the seeking of refuge from a common enemy, seeking a place where we do not have to make hard decisions for ourselves, or where there will be others to help us get through, taking some of the responsibility and its associated stress. We also may seek communal relationships in an effort to deepen our relationship as corporate members with our God and to more effectively serve Him by serving others. Searches for answers in the available literature regarding the how-to of setting up a commune tend to stress things like choosing participants, setting the goals, organising, establishing rituals and procedures, writing by-laws, and finding funding sources.

While these, and many other, practical concerns may appear to be appropriate for communes, they often sound more like society formation than commune nurturing, and they also do not apply so much to the development of communal living in a Christian context. In the Church, and its many sub-branch congregations, the members are not selected by a human individual or group; many of the structures and organisational features are either given in Scripture or have been handed down through history. Further, Church members generally do not live together and share things in common as in monastic living, nor do we have a long history of village communal living, as mentioned in the examples earlier in the chapter. It would appear, then, that deep communion in the holistic sense of a deep relationship between individuals who are willing to give up their individuality is something of an ideal. This ideal is not beyond reach, but experience shows that if attained, in most instances, it may not be long-lived. For most of us, our commitment to commune, apart from our inherent self-centeredness, will be divided due to our family, extended family, and work responsibilities, and these will probably render a true, twenty-four-seven commune impossible.

---

[31] Ephesians 4:13
[32] Bonhoeffer, 1954

In addition to these caveats, there are some other factors that should be mentioned. The first, and perhaps obvious one, is the problem of withdrawal from the world, a world with which we are called to engage and to which we are called to be witnesses of the Truth. Of course, as mentioned in the last chapter, it is possible to structure a communal, or monastic, existence so that the communal relationships, or the monastery, become beacons of light in a dark world. Another important point arises as a result of the increase in individualism through the objectification of the world in the post-Enlightenment age. This means that we do not see or feel ourselves to be an indivisible part of reality anymore. While the communal, deep relationships may seem in some ways to be the ideal, that type of communalism perhaps might not afford us the ability to step back in a super-objectivist way and see the big picture. It might, however, give us a small hint as to what reality might look like from God's perspective.

9. Further Features of the Relationship Categories

In this chapter, we will look briefly at just some of the other features of the relational series categories. As we have said, for the purposes of the series model, each is being seen as somewhat discrete, but there appears to be evidence of each one existing wherever human beings live in close proximity. The different facets of our relationality evidence themselves in our perspectives on the world, in our self-definition, and in the way we treat others. For individualists, all others are outsiders, but the othering of others is a feature of all the relational groups, where other groups are seen to be outsiders, and the identity of group members is tied closely to the type, structure and function of the group.

The commonalities across the categories, such as the range of relationships with others, may vary in degree and type to give each a particular 'flavour', and many of these have already been mentioned. There are many other examples of this, but to take one, research by Yūki and Brewer[1] found that members of individualistic and collectivist cultures tended to exhibit the same degree of idiocentric (centring on the self) self-descriptions in terms of group membership. Collectivists tended to see themselves more in terms of membership of small groups, while individualists saw themselves generally as being part of larger groups.

Another example is the use of venerative speech. It is probably true to say that in all cultures, there are words, grammatical constructions, or communication formats that are used to indicate either the depth of a relationship or a perceived social status difference that exists between two people. (This, of course, is an important consideration when we try to communicate or relate cross-culturally.) And just to complicate matters further, Moemeka noted that in different cultures: "Not only are members concerned about their messages reaching their destinations and meeting the needs for which they were sent, they are more concerned about how the result of their communication would affect existing and potential future human relationships."[2] Relational language and the showing of respect become important means by which a

---

[1] Yūki & Brewer, 2014
[2] Moemeka, 1998, p. 124

group ethos and order are maintained, and they also play a role to limit intra-group conflict.[3]

The indicative forms of speech in Spanish were mentioned in Chapter 2 with regard to collectivist relationships (the use of the formal, *usted* or familiar, *tu* for the English 'you'). Within the hierarchical structures of African communal contexts venerative speech codes are much more developed. The familiarity that we express in the West often appears to be missing. Musa[4] mentioned that in some contexts it is insulting for younger siblings to refer to an older sibling by their first name. Addressing others appropriately will involve the use of formal names, clan identities and ancestral names, as well as informal names, such as nicknames, and this helps cement the relational structure within the group. In practice, greetings, therefore, can take a considerable time and may involve the recitation of a Praise Poem. This affirms the Zulu concept of *Sawubona*, "I see you", while at the same time, recognising that your essence is beyond the visible. Pearson (in Musa) suggested that embedded in this traditional greeting is the idea that "I see your personality. I see your humanity. I see your dignity and respect."[5] The rules that form the basis of the venerative speech codes are critical to maintaining the structure of the group. Musa claimed that there are aspects of venerative speech code in Western and Asian contexts through its implied respect and recognition of the other.

> [In African contexts]. . . it encompasses many African cultural norms that are essentially integral to African worldview, values, and traditions. It is rooted in the African view of the human and the relationships between the self, community, and the cosmos. It is rooted in African essentialism . . . . Venerative speech code is a mode of communication in which the speaker affirms the beingness of the other by speaking in terms that edify, dignify, enrich, esteem, and value the other. It is demonstrated in the address, salutation, and exchange between members of the community. It is also evident in the indirect speech, use of proverbs, poetics, and conspiracy of meaning to promote mutuality and common good (Musa 2005). Venerative speech codes theory is a performative theory. The theory sees speech as enacted interactivity in which past experiences, present realities, and future expectations dictate the dance of social exchange. The one gives full veneration to the other, not in an instrumental sense, but in authentic regard for the ultimate being of the other. Veneration is inspired by the sense of awe one feels in the presence of majesty, royalty, and transcendence. Except that

---

[3] Jagers & Mock, 1995
[4] Musa, 2017
[5] Musa, 2017, p. 118

in this case, it is not reserved for the spectacular or the extraordinary. It is offered to others, whom one even would regard as "ordinary", so to speak. It is the manifestation of the belief that there is no such thing as an "ordinary" individual.[6]

This then begs the questions for us as egalitarian, Western individualists: What venerative speech is used in our groupings? Is it even considered necessary? In Christian organisations, how do organisation members refer to those in what we call leadership positions? How do leaders speak to others in the organisation? Of course, it may also be that if venerative speech code is used, it may be from the heart as a genuinely felt respect, or simply a part of the organisational culture with which an individual feels they must conform because it is a practice that those in authority have decreed. An example of this would be the use of saluting in the military.

Of course, the veneration offered may come in the form also of subtle body language—for example, a slight nod of the head or a hand gesture towards a better seat. Given our relational awkwardness as independent, individualists, who see ourselves as being egalitarian and free from class distinctions, such gestures are given at times with an almost sarcastic air or over-exaggeration. Within collectivist and communalist cultures, hierarchical structures (what we in the West might call 'class' differentials) are seen as essential elements that provide a high degree of cohesion for the group. Within many individualistic cultures, with our emphasis on egalitarianism, such class structuring of a society may appear abhorrent, and we may look with some bemusement at the class structures of some European countries and askance at the caste system in India.

As egalitarian as we may feel, we do develop our own systems within countries and organisations. We do not expect school students to speak to the school principal using the principal's first name. In most businesses and organisations, including Christian ones, we feel that respect and the associated venerative speech codes, mild as they often may be, will help to support an organisational structure of sorts. In the West, it becomes much more of a personal issue. Some may feel that it would help them to know where they 'fit' in the organisation. Some with earned titles, such as Doctor or Professor (in the UK sense), may ask that the title never be used when spoken to, while others may insist on it. At times, however, the hierarchical structures and the associated venerative speech to be used are needed to provide a degree of control, given our fallen human natures and our inclination to do the wrong thing. Human fallen nature leads very naturally to a greed for power. We struggle as individuals with our position in the cosmos, and a desire to control others is never far away. Much has been written

---

[6] Ibid., p. 109

on this topic, but we might give just one related Scripture reference from Revelation 5. In John's apocalyptic vision he sees and hears the Heavenly hosts and all of Creation:

> In a loud voice they sang: "Worthy is the Lamb, who was slain, to receive power and wealth and wisdom and strength and honor and glory and praise!" Then I heard every creature in heaven and on earth and under the earth and on the sea, and all that is in them, singing: "To him who sits on the throne and to the Lamb be praise and honor and glory and power, for ever and ever!" (Revelation 5:12–13)

The things that are attributed to God by them in this venerative speech act—power, wealth, wisdom, strength, honour, glory, and praise—are the very things we, as individuals, crave for ourselves and have desired through all of human history since the Garden of Eden—our desire to be like God. It is not surprising then, that so often human beings seek the venerative speech references that are due to God alone.

Further distinctions

Rather than a structured, corporate sense of being, in Western cultures, it is the collective will of individuals that unites for community or for communal purposes. Particularly for community membership, this, in a sense, is a safe stance for us as we feel that we can join or leave at will without redefining our personhood too much. This is different from tribal village cultures or strong communal cultures. In these settings, to leave the group is to lose one's identity. This is exemplified in African contexts: "In African communalism, communal life is the very foundation and centre of human life from which the human person emerges."[7]

Fowler noted, however, that communalism, as practised in African cultures, was not without its defects or distortions of humanness. The obscuring of individual personhood, he argued, actually inhibits the healthy development of the group as a whole, and the tightness of the groups often prevents cross-group communications and knowledge development. The inhibition of individuality, however, may be seen also in individualistic contexts:

> In a similar way, Western individualism, by obscuring human communality, not only blocks an effective experience of communality but suppresses the effective expression of human individuality. Lacking an experience of authentic community, the Western world finds pale substitutes for communal life in organized group activities. These communal substitutes, in the interests of the organizational efficiency and control, press the human person into organizational molds of conformity that inhibit individuality.[8]

---

[7] Fowler, 1993, p. 20
[8] Ibid., p. 21

Of course, the fact that as individualists we feel the importance of the individual, independent self, does not mean that there is no attraction felt for a deep relationship with others. Often, that desire may be to relationships with single individuals or very small groups, such as groups of friends who meet to chat, go fishing, or play golf. These would hardly count as communes, but they are indicative of our desire for a deep relationship with others. In 1782, the French émigré to North America, Hector Crèvecoeur, was puzzled that thousands of European colonists had "become Indians", leaving their European way of life behind. He wrote: "There must be in their social bond something singularly captivating and far superior to anything to be boasted of among us."[9] The seeking of the communal, tribal life over European ways, however, may not be quite as straightforward as selecting communalism over individualism. It might be noted that, first, the colonists themselves must have had a communal way of life as they banded together against the elements and perceived or real enemies. Second, Benjamin Franklin, in a letter written in 1753, noted that the carefree lifestyle of the Indians, hunting and fishing where game was plentiful, and with little other labor, contrasted with the struggle to survive and build that was the life of the colonists.[10] This illustrates that very frequently, there are multiple factors that influence our choices regarding group membership and depth of relationship.

All of that said, we exist in multiple relational frameworks, or categories, and as Fowler has noted, we really should not be attempting to self-define ourselves as individuals, nor as integral, communal elements. Rather, "we are defined in the infinitely rich multifaceted complex of human personhood by the Lord our God."[11] This portrayal of human beings denies the alternatives as definitions of being; rather, they become attributes. In the place of a so-defined individual, a human person has God-given individuality, and instead of a communal element, a person has God-given communality. This is illustrated, as mentioned, in the Pauline descriptive metaphor of the body, where no part may function without the whole and yet each functions individually. There are various metaphorical references in the New Testament to the unified Body of Christ. For example, Peter speaks of us being "like living stones" that "are being built into a spiritual house to be a holy priesthood" (1 Peter 2:5a). Paul is taken with body imagery:

> Instead, speaking the truth in love, we will in all things grow up into him who is the Head, that is, Christ. From him the whole body, joined and held together

---

[9] Crèvecoeur, 2103, p. 161
[10] Sparks, 1840
[11] Fowler, 1993, p. 22

by every supporting ligament, grows and builds itself up in love, as each part does its work.[12]

Therefore each of you must put off falsehood and speak truthfully to his neighbor, for we are all members of one body.

The body is a unit, though it is made up of many parts; and though all its parts are many, they form one body. So it is with Christ. For we were all baptized by one Spirit into one body—whether Jews or Greeks, slave or free—and we were all given the one Spirit to drink. Now the body is not made up of one part but of many. If the foot should say, "Because I am not a hand, I do not belong to the body," it would not for that reason cease to be part of the body. And if the ear should say, "Because I am not an eye, I do not belong to the body," it would not for that reason cease to be part of the body. If the whole body were an eye, where would the sense of hearing be? If the whole body were an ear, where would the sense of smell be? But in fact, God has arranged the parts in the body, every one of them, just as he wanted them to be. If they were all one part, where would the body be? As it is, there are many parts, but one body.[13]

In the current consideration of the components of our relational series, it is important to recognise several things from these metaphors from both Peter and Paul. First, the buildings and bodies speak to a wholeness, an indivisible, physical unity, an *ubuntu*, 'I am because we are' but also a 'we are because He is'. Second, while the house and the body are entities in themselves, they are made up of individuals, each having its own identity and not melded together inseparably like the cream in homogenised milk. Third, the individuals are not the house or the body. They are only the building blocks and small parts that can never take to themselves the glory of the whole. In the end of all things, it is about the house or the body, not about the stones and body parts. So, God deals with His human beings on two levels, as individuals and as a unified, and becoming more unified, whole. The first three chapters of the book of Revelation were written to the seven churches in Asia Minor—letters to congregations. And yet, in Revelation 3:23, we have Jesus speaking to "any<u>one</u>", singular. So, before God, we are independent individuals but also members of communities, collectives, and perhaps communes, but, above all, members of a covenant-bonded unity with a spiritual dimension beyond our understanding at present.

The meaning of "independent" here is that man's covenantal standing before God is not dependent in any way of his belonging to a human group or collective—family, local church, genetic, ethnic, or national entity, social

---

[12] Ephesians 4:15–16; 4:25
[13] 1 Corinthians 12:12–20

stratum or status, professional guild, political party, etc. While belonging to or [having] membership in any such entity or collective may be an important *secondary* or *inferior cause* (to borrow Calvin's terminology) for a man's willingness to obey God, or for his training to good works, in the final account, God deals with man according to man's individual standing before God, without any regard for any collectives he may have been part of.[14]

Of course, despite Marinov's final statement, there is one "collective" before God that for us is of ultimate importance and that is the membership, bought with the redeeming sacrifice of God's Son: His Church.

Worldview assumptions

Earlier, we mentioned the objectification or reality that has been a particular feature of Western civilisations since the Enlightenment. We engage with reality by standing back and observing it with some level of detachment. This idea of seeing the world objectively led Emanuel Kant to use the German word *Weltanschauung*, literally, in English translation, worldview, and we mentioned this in Chapter one. This objectification, aided by the rationalism of the Age of Reason, has been a critical feature of the scientific revolution and naturalism. In its simplest form, it implies just looking at objects around us, but at a deeper level, it means that reality is seen as only those things that can be seen. Only those things that can be measured in a laboratory, as the saying goes, are real. This has been a convenient perspective to advocate for the denial of the existence of God, of course.

There are other ways by which we engage with reality but not every culture, however, has a world 'view'. Given their objectivity, with regard to the relationality series, we may assume that individualists have a worldview. At the other end, communalists may be said to have a world-*feel*. They *sense* the holistic physical and non-physical environment. As Oyewum explained,

> The term "worldview", which is used in the West to sum up the cultural logic of a society, captures the West's privileging of the visual. It is Eurocentric to use it to describe cultures that may privilege other senses. The term "world-sense" is a more inclusive way of describing the conception of the world by different cultural groups.[15]

As well as worldview and world-sense assumptions, some cultures have been described as having a world-*hear*[16], or a *feel-think*[17], and we might ponder how the

---

[14] Marinov, 2018, para. 3
[15] Oyewum, 2016, pp.2–3
[16] Ong, 1968
[17] Cepeda, 2017; Escobar, 2016

different relationality categories engage with reality in these terms. It would seem that for modern individualists, those for whom the affective domain pair mentioned below is pleasure-pain, it would probably be something like a world-affectively-experienced. In societist structures, it may be divided between an individual worldview (in the West) and a view mediated to a greater or lesser extent by the structure, purposes, and leadership of the society. For collectivities, the assumptions pertaining to 'reality' are developed and mediated by the ingroup core. These ideas also beg the question for us regarding the presentation of the Gospel to those in the World—a strikingly cross-cultural pursuit.

The importance of relationality and our affective domains

The idea of the importance of honour and shame in some cultures has been mentioned in the chapter on collectivism. Since Ruth Benedict's research in Japan, many others have studied aspects of what became known as shame-honour and guilt-innocence cultures, sometimes referring to them as shame and guilt cultures, though the negativity of those designations should be avoided. In general terms, the honour cultures are the collectivist cultures, and the individualistic cultures tend to be more interested in justice and innocence. Two other affective domain distinctions identified in cultures are the pairs, fear-power[18] and pain-pleasure.[19] The cultures that make a particular priority of seeking power and avoiding fear tend to be the animistic tribal-communalist cultures, whereas in more recent years in the West, there has been a significant move towards pleasure seeking and the avoidance of pain in its various forms. While these distinctions are only one way by which cultures may be examined, the four pairs are evident in all cultures, but the different cultures prioritise the importance of the pairs differently.

Work by Roland Muller,[20] Benjamin Hegeman,[21] and others has suggested that there is a correlation between religious beliefs and the affective domain pairs. Research by Beech[22] indicated that the link was not causal with regard to religious beliefs (specifically of Christians, Moslems, and animists—and one might now add atheistic individualists). Rather, the priorities given by different cultures tended to be related directly to relationship frameworks. These relational frameworks then either fitted a particular set of religious beliefs or beliefs were adapted, or syncretised, to be accommodated into the relational framework. This is a complex area that may be studied, but the following very brief points may be useful.

---

[18] Muller, 2006; Blaschke, 2002
[19] Beech, 2011; Hegeman, 2006
[20] Muller, 2006
[21] Hegeman, 2006
[22] Beech, 2011

<u>Pair omnipresence</u>: Before considering the four pairs separately, we should note that guilt, shame, fear and pain, as well as innocence, honour, power and pleasure are to be found throughout Scripture. We see them evident in the account of the first humans made in God's image, in the story of God's people, Israel, in the life, ministry, death, resurrection, and ascension of Christ, in the accounts of the early Church, and in the Parousia. These are fundamental feelings for created-in-God's-image, but fallen, human beings, and we see evidence of them all around us.

Modern individualism is the relating of the self to the self while possibly neglecting other forms of relationality. We have already mentioned the fourth pair, pleasure and pain, in modern Western societies where comfort seeking and pain avoidance are prioritised. The hedonism that is portrayed in the media and sought in practice has always been with fallen human beings, but its ranking in the prioritisation seems to have risen in recent years as the importance of the *I* has grown. Succeeding generations are finding more drugs and other distractions to gain pleasure sensations and to remove as much physical, emotional, psychological, or spiritual pain as possible. It becomes all about *me*.

The ranking of these affective domain pairs also has implications for the communication and reception of the Gospel message. Individualists, with the emphasis on guilt feelings, have been preached a Gospel of forgiveness of sins—perhaps using so-called guilt-tripping messages. We assume in the West that the Gospel is a Gospel of salvation from sin, but if we look through the Scriptures with less-Western eyes, we see that, yes, Christ came to save us from the consequences of sin, and our broken relationship with God, but also He came to save us from shame, fear and pain of different types. As mentioned earlier, collectivist cultures may be more likely to accept or reject the Gospel as a group (particularly a family group) than as individuals. Communal animists, as Blaschke has pointed out, seek a God who can protect them from the other 'powers' that they fear, and this means that they may be very willing to accept Christ as 'Lord' before they become aware of their sin and need of Him as Saviour. For non-animist communal groups, often there is a fear of impending danger from outside that has been the impetus for commencing the group, and working as a single unit provides the power to resist feared attacks from outside. These groups also may respond more willingly to a Gospel presenting Jesus as Lord first. The final group, prioritising pleasure and pain, seeks some spiritual being or experience that will provide them with feelings of pleasure or at least well-being, such that they can feel good about themselves and their lives. A false "prosperity Gospel" is well suited to this group, which does not wish to feel guilty or ashamed, but may be enticed by the possibility of some wealth and comfort, sounds like reassurances.

To give an illustration of the different ways those from other cultures may view the Gospel, and taken from Bob Blaschke's *Quest for Power: Guidelines for Communicating the Gospel to Animists,* from his time working in West Africa he wrote:

> Here is the account of the happening in the village of Salonzi where prior to the presentation of the Gospel most of the young to middle aged men had already made a group decision to convert to Islam. Then along came a group of young Boko called Christians singing and announcing the good news of Jesus Christ. One of the talks had to do with John 14:6b, where Jesus says ". . . no one comes to the Father except through me." The Holy Spirit burdened these villagers with the thought that there is only one way to get to God or heaven, the Jesus way. These men believed they had already taken God's way in Islam, but they were perplexed that there might possibly be another way. Reasoning that they could only be one true way they decided to settle the matter on a hunt.
>
> They designated the kill of a roan antelope to be indicative that Islam was true way. If they got a hartebeest then they would know that the Jesus Way was the true way. Let me insert here that the roan are the more numerous, less cautious and therefore easier to hunt. By the end of the day on this hunt they had killed two hartebeests, no roan. The dilemma was indisputably resolved; they all rejected Islam and took the Jesus Way. The spiritual power encounter revealed to them the belief system which was more powerful, therefore the true way. From now on they were 'Jesus people'.[23]

In a personal conversation, Bob Blaschke recounted that these people visited him in the seminary where he was teaching and said to him, "We are Christians now. What do we have to do?" The hartebeests had settled the matter. Jesus was obviously Lord, and they could accept Him as such. It would take further instruction to show them that there was a sin problem, for which they would have felt little or no guilt, that had to be dealt with as well. This wishing to relate to Jesus as Lord prior to accepting Him as sin-Saviour is the reverse of the order proclaimed in the West, but it is one that is quite natural in some other cultural contexts. In the presentation of a holistic Gospel, none of the things we are saved from or to should be ignored, and a teaching that overemphasises only one of them can lead to heresy. An example of this may be a strict law-based fundamentalism in the West.

A similar point may be made with all the relational categories. All of them may be found in all cultural settings, though they will be prioritised differently. To concentrate solely on one and ignore the influence of the others, in any setting, is to misunderstand

---

[23] Blaschke, 2001, p. 88

the relationship structures within the group. To think that in our Western cultures only individualism exists and all should be treated only as individuals is to miss the importance of the other relationship categories that will exist and shape the lives of culture members. This, then, leads us to consider the implications involving the pairs with regard to the items on our relational category series and the following questions may be asked when working with individuals:

- In an individualistic culture, what things induce guilt and how do they think guilt feelings may be assuaged? Do the structures within which they work appear fair and promote justice so that guilt and innocence in any situation are clearly distinguished?

- With a collectivist group, how are shame and honour generated and expressed? Are both the generation and the expression appropriate biblically?

- With a communal group, what is feared and what power is sought to limit the fear? Is it purely internal to the group, or is it the trust in God?

As mentioned, we are very familiar with teaching that emphasises the fact that we should feel guilty for what we have and have not done, and that is usually the way individualists approach the Gospel. If we consider a Christian group, or sub-group, as having collectivist attributes, then shame is something that is felt by group members when a transgression is exposed to the group, but, more importantly, this includes the 'parental core' of the collective: the all-seeing, all-knowing God the Father. In a similar way, Christian groups acting communally must be relying on the power of God and not human groupness for peace of mind.

Compulsory communing

A final, brief note in this chapter concerns the compulsory formation of communion. Mention has already been made of the formation and rule of communist states over the past century or so. While the original, and particularly the early, Lutheran-inspired ideas, of Karl Marx[24] may have had some admirable qualities in terms of caring for the poor and limiting the human greed, Marx seemed to have missed the point that we are 'fallen' human beings and those who tried, or said they tried, to put his teaching into practice, found that the implementation had to be forced. Bringing people together to work together in harmony to achieve goals for the advancement of all on a national scale had to be brought into being by total and brutal subjugation, in what we know as communism. Not all of the forced bringing together of humans to live and work in close proximity in activities that might be described as communal, however, has been on the

---

[24] Marx's university paper, *The Union of Believers With Christ According to John 15: 1-14, Showing its Basis and Essence, its Absolute Necessity, and its Effects*, gives an interesting insight into some of his thinking at the time.

left of politics. There have been many other forms for many reasons. The following example, taken from right-wing-inspired events in World War II, may give pause for thought, particularly for those in positions of leadership in a group.

Bojidar Marinov summarised sections of Bruno Bettelheim's[25] work, *The Informed Heart: Autonomy in a Mass Age*, where Bettelheim reflects on the means by which forced cohesion was established in the punitive systems applied by Nazi Germany during World War II and within Iron Curtain countries shortly after. Bettelheim, a Freudian psychologist, had observed first-hand the suffering of prisoners under the Nazis in the Dachau and Buchenwald concentration camps. Marinov's definition of collectivity is not the same as the one used in this work, but his citing of Bettleheim was to illustrate the destruction of individuality in forms of forced grouping. In other words, the following procedures were used, apart from the more obvious torture and deprivation, and intended to create group cohesion in order to more easily manipulate the group. As we read them, we may reflect on any of them that may be evident in the groups within which we relate to others.

1. Useless work. This included the arduous task of repeatedly moving piles of heavy stones to another place and then moving them back, or the digging of trenches with bare hands when shovels were nearby but could not be used. Such work was soul-destroying and induced insanity in many and suicide in some. This contrasted with the work of those who made munitions, where they continued their production, even if they were shown films of the destruction their work caused in their home countries. At least their work had some purpose.

2. The giving of multiple, perhaps even mutually exclusive, commands. This has been used in many situations with prisoners of war, where a rapidly delivered series of commands that may make no sense are given, and strict obedience is required. This is also a technique in which many police are trained so that when encountering a dangerous situation, such as with an armed assailant, compliance may be gained through the assailant becoming confused.

3. Collective responsibility. Making the group responsible for the sins of an individual is not a new phenomenon. It was practised in Roman armies, where one in ten (as in the word, decimation) would be killed by the others if a group had shown cowardice or had deserted. It also brings to mind the sin of Achan following the attack on Ai (Joshua 7) and also imputed 'original sin'.

4. Removal of personal moral responsibility. Our human nature involves a strong moral sense, and we grow to understand that some things justly deserve a reward and some justly deserve punishment. Where the judgments relating to these are removed from the individual and applied in a random and unjust manner, confusion reigns. As

---

[25] Bettelheim, 1979

Bettelheim observed, the Jews in the camps who were abused for just being Jews, were able to withstand the abuse better psychologically than some others because they at least knew why they were being abused.

5. The refusal to see injustice. By rewarding group members for ignoring injustice committed against an individual, they may become blind to injustice, or at least not react to it. Marinov cites instances within the police forces in the USA where individual members of the force have perpetrated a crime (for example, shooting and killing an unarmed civilian), and other members of the force do nothing and may react strongly against anyone who complains.

6. The transgression of our moral boundaries. Once injustices are ignored, then a further step is forcing or encouraging someone to step over the line of their morality. There have been many horrendous instances of this in wartime, but it is a common practice in many societies today. The important feature of this is that for someone to come completely under the control of another, a dictator, a god, or an institution, for example, there needs to be rebellion against God and His moral order. For the Phoenicians, for example, to bring all under the power of the god Molech (King), parents were required to break their moral boundaries by sacrificing their own children.

In the West, unless we live in monastic isolation, we probably will all have been in forced community or communal situations. These may be due to the necessity of work, or social pressures or, as in the case of compulsory school education, by government decree. And by desire, default or decree, many of us will have been in positions of leadership, authority or governance of such groups. As we observe, or dictate, the functioning of the group, do we see evidence of: 'Useless' work being required; multiple, perhaps even mutually exclusive, commands being given; collective responsibility being stipulated; personal moral responsibility being removed; a refusal to see injustice; or the 'forced' transgression of moral boundaries? Hopefully, we do not live or work in situations as dire as Nazi Germany, but some or all of these may be evident in some subtle way in our organisations. For school teachers, one must wonder about 'busy work' given to students at times, the punishment of a class for some individual's offence, instructions given too quickly or using language not easily understood, or effectively forcing a student to lie when being pressed with questions about some misdemeanour.

10. Putting it Together

In concluding this book, we want to look at some further implications of our human tendency to relatedness within a biblical framework. While earlier, we distinguished the term 'community' from the other relational frameworks and gave it a specific meaning, we know that the term is used in very general ways, often as something of a catch-all term referring to many different types of voluntary groupings of human beings. Often, it is used positively, implying some type of ideal state of human relations and hence the quantity of literature related to community formation and maintenance.

Relating to God

As the written word, the Bible may be used in many ways. Apart from its misuse to provide backing for a spurious argument, it may be used for moral guidance, or to highlight examples of Godly and un-Godly living, and so forth. Fundamentally, however, the Bible contains a story, God's story, and a significant purpose of the Bible is to draw us into its story . . . a story of God and God's people. It draws us in, individually and collectively, to a story of deep relationship with God and deep relationships between His people. But the priority is always to be our relationship with Him. We are to be allegiant to the 'core' by the work of the Holy Spirit, bringing oneness.

This relationship with God, however, must be His work, whether it is seen in terms of an individual relating, a society, a community, a collective, or a commune. He is altogether other: holy. This otherness of God, utterly beyond all other otherness, of course, makes it an easy matter for fallen human beings to reject Him and maintain what they believe to be a clear conscience. The gods of the Greeks, Romans, and even many cultures today, whether comprised of idols, spirits of ancestors, superheroes, or some other deity form, are other in the sense of being imagined as being in some way human-plus. These gods have provided a core around which humans are able to gather and relate to each other through commonly held beliefs. In recent centuries, Western individualists have worked diligently at the creation of made-in-there-own-image-gods, manageable gods that may be kept close and whose characteristics may be changed as needed. Unlike the culturally-bound gods, these gods are personal and are purported to operate at the whim of the individual.

Similarities and differences

As we have looked at the -isms (individualism, societism, etc.) in the relational series, we have seen that there are elements of each in perhaps any grouping of human beings. They all feature a form of relationship that we have and are all grounded in 'being'. That is, they all contribute to our sense of what it means to 'be' as human 'be'-ings. While there may be evidence of a dominance of one type of relationality over another, no group is exclusively defined by only one, though we use the terms as generalisations. There are commonalities across all of them, and members of all will evidence goal seeking, whether it be an individual's goals or those of a commune. Perhaps with rare exceptions, we all will seek such universals as justice, security, achievement, well-being, peaceful coexistence, care of parents for children, and so on. The differences appear in how these things are perceived and achieved within the different relational frameworks. In practical terms, then, it may prove helpful for us to be aware of the different relationship structures at work in the groups within which we find ourselves or with which we work. This involves seeing the blend of frameworks and how these fit together.

Whether a group in which we are involved is a Christian education institution, a church congregation, or some other Christian organisation, there will be group members who operate largely as individuals, others complying with a society structure, others who see themselves as community members, and so on. What might be the proportion of each within the group, and what gives the group its defining relationality? Many times in Christian groups, very significant conflicts can arise as one person or a sub-group sees themselves relating in a different way from others. By way of a simple example, an individualist may want to assert their personal view on a point of doctrine, while a societist will try to abide by the 'rules', a communitarian may want to 'just get along', a collectivist will tend to form part of a tight group around an individual and will try to distinguish their beliefs from those they see as outgroups and not trust them, and a communalist will be frustrated by the lack of depth of relationship within the group! As the title of this book indicates, the ideal of what is broadly termed community, even Christian community, can be quite elusive.

Of course, as Christians, we know that it's not all about us. God has His way of using us, individually or as a group, for His purposes. Some years ago, a small church that was temporarily without a pastor was experiencing very significant relational difficulties that might be described as all of the above, and with strong personalities involved as well. Early one Sunday morning, the church secretary received a call from a woman in a town an hour's drive away. She said that her husband had cancer and he wanted to go to church one last time before becoming bedridden. They had been in the town a few months before to meet friends in another church, but that church service was not being conducted, so they had attended this one, as it were, by 'accident'. The reason they wanted to attend on this Sunday, despite the hour's drive, was that they said they had felt an amazing peace in the church. This came as something of a shock to the church secretary! It transpired, however, that the cancer sufferer was not a Christian but became one shortly after their visit. God had overridden the relationality issues for His purposes.

This necessary emphasis on the centre of our Christian community building is highlighted further by Martin Buber:

> The true community does not arise through people having feelings for one another (though indeed not without it), but through, first, their taking their stand in living mutual relation with a living Centre, and, second, their being in living mutual relation with one another. The second has its source in the first, but is not given when the first alone is given. Living mutual relation includes feelings, but does not originate with them. The community is built up out of living mutual relation, but the builder is the living effective-Centre.[1]

We usually see our Christian 'institutions' as communities, even 'communities of faith', or at least communities of faithful practice. Yet whether we aim for commune or community, problems arise: primarily problems that derive from human nature as individuals seek to have their own way. We resist being vulnerable to others. We avoid accountability where possible. We 'other' others or outgroups, separating ourselves from them for a range of reasons. When we do clump together, it may be due to tribal instincts drawing us together against a common threat or enemy. At the same time, we all too often see ourselves as so many north poles of magnets, and therefore, we drive each other apart. And yet, a Christian community should be where we train to be Christlike, learning to love to the extent that we would be willing to give our lives for those we most cherish, and to be accountable to others: "Community is woven through *love-drenched accountability*."[2] The vulnerability and accountability required must come from God by the work of His Holy Spirit in our lives.

Given the human tendency to live together in relationship, the commands in Scripture to do so, and the continuing battle we have with our fallen natures, perhaps it is not surprising that Christian communities, of different sorts, rise and fall. By way of a simple allegory, we might consider attempts to sustain community in terms of an orchestra. When listening to orchestral music, most of us can identify a melody, and we may be able to identify harmony structures. It is probably beyond the most sophisticated listener, however, to be able to identify the playing of, say, the third, second violinist in a symphonic piece—as long as the player is playing in accordance with the conducted score. If one of the third violinists were not playing, then we probably

---

[1] Buber, 2018, p. 45
[2] Brookes, 2019, p. 73

would not notice, though the harmony quality could be diminished. The intent of the symphonic composer is the production of a blended harmony of many voices, in which individual voices may be indistinguishable. The whole becomes greater than the sum of its parts. Or at least, qualitatively different. At times, the composer may feature one instrument playing a theme or a variation, and at other times another instrument, but the whole performance must blend seamlessly together. Of course, it only takes that third, second violinist to play the wrong notes, and the whole effect is no longer perfect. It seems then that perhaps individuals seeking community can sometimes appear to be like musicians playing their own seemingly random notes against an orchestral background, trying, without a score, endeavouring, at least sometimes, to fit in . . . but at the same time, as individualists, still desiring to have their sound recognised above the rest. Perhaps they know the music's key, at least, and therefore improve their chances of hitting a correct note. Or perhaps they simply play the same note repeatedly, hoping that at least at some points they will engage with the harmony.

The Church

Many have been concerned with the decline in church attendance in recent decades, with its attendant decline in Christians relating to each other, and this has usually been seen as an indicator of a falling away from Christianity. This, however, may not be the case, or at least not the entire explanation. Robert Putnam,[3] in his evocatively titled, *Bowling Alone*, has mapped research on the membership in the USA of a wide range of clubs and associations. The results show a rise in the early years of the last century, a fall in the 1930s, a strong rise around World War II years, and since the mid-1950s, a significant decline each year. So, not only has church attendance been declining in the USA, but membership in all forms of sociation that require some level of commitment. At first glance, this may generate a sigh of relief for Christians, but on reflection, it may indicate that in many cases churches may have functioned in the past as something like a club or association rather than as the unique Body of Christ—or at least many of those attending may have seen their attendance in those terms.

This has been the case particularly in the so-called Christian countries where Christianity has been, by decree or *de facto,* a State religion or at least strongly supported by the State or particularly powerful political parties. In the mid-19th century, the Danish philosopher, Søren Kierkegaard, was cutting in his writings concerning the church in Denmark, which was aligned with, and supported by, the government. He decried such a club-ish institution that had drifted so far from the Gospel message of

---

[3] Putnam, 2000

Jesus and the cost of discipleship that it entails. He wrote scathingly concerning the church hierarchy, where he saw hypocrisy and an attention to wealth accumulation.

In these contexts, we can but wonder about some current-day church groups. The cost of discipleship, of becoming a member of Jesus' Church, may be high, and seemingly higher for some than for others, and when we compare that with the attainment of comfort and pleasure, we may say it is too much. When the interpersonal relationships in Christian life are defined by feel-good sermons, cozy chats with friends on a Sunday morning, pot-luck suppers, and a general feeling that we are doing OK, then, as Kierkegaard proclaimed, there is something wrong with the church. And if that is the case, then we can expect attendance to decline as membership of all clubs and associations decline as our cultures forge their way deeper into individualism.

"Face-to-face conversation is the most human and humanizing thing."[4] Yet the irony in an increasingly individualistic situation is that we do not seem to have made the connection between reducing face-to-face engagement with other human beings and deepening feelings of loneliness. Often people seem to know they are lonely but don't seem to understand why. Many organisations have been established to try to understand and alleviate the problem, and governments are taking notice as well. In the United Kingdom in 2018, the Prime Minister, following a report by a commission showing 20% of people in Britain claimed to feel lonely, added "Loneliness" to the remit of the government's Ministry for Sport and Civil Society. A Cigna survey[5] of over 20,000 adults in the United States concluded that loneliness had reached 'epidemic levels' in the US:

> Almost half of people said they sometimes or always feel alone or left out, 43% said they sometimes or always feel that their relationships are not meaningful and only 53% said they have meaningful in-person interactions on a daily basis.[6]

Not only has our deepening engagement with individualism led to a sense of isolation and loneliness, but, as David Brookes has seen, in a retreat from loneliness, it also may give rise to a form of tribalism. This may have been an unexpected phenomenon, but we see evidence of it all around us today. We appear to be only individuals pragmatically—driven by our wills, desires and loves. When there is a perceived threat, we can become tribal very quickly. The tribalism that has grown is not a communal tribalism based on shared identity and strong bonding in love to others, but one based on protection against a common enemy, or perhaps a perceived enemy.

---

[4] Turkle, 2015, p. 3
[5] Cigna, 2020
[6] Ducharme, 2018, para. 5

> Tribalists seek out easy categories in which some people are good and others are bad. They seek out certainty to conquer their feelings of unbearable doubt. The seek out war—political war or actual war—as a way to give life meaning. They revert to tribe. Tribalism seems like a way to restore the bonds of community. It certainly does bind people together. But it is actually the dark twin of community. Community is connection based on mutual affection. Tribalism, in the sense I'm using here, is connection based on mutual hatred. Community is based on common humanity; tribalism on common foe.[7]

The ignoring of Jesus' commands to love, that we see in this form of tribalism, is, after all, evidence of the dehumanising efforts that the Enemy of humankind seeks to engender not only in those made in God's image in general, but particularly in His Church. Tribalistic othering by Christians has always been a part of the Church (for example, the difficulties relating to the distinctions between Christian Jews and gentile Christians in the first century), but it is something that should be resisted if we are to be true to Christ's Gospel. The very example given by Jesus makes this clear. Jesus was interested in and demanded a commitment to Himself first and foremost. (This may be a difficult, long-term path, particularly for younger generations in the West, the 'options' generations, where choices are made based on a temporary situation . . . until something better comes along.) Once that commitment had been secured, relationality, despite differences, became a given. He called a tax collector for the Romans, an anti-Rome zealot, and His betrayer, to be part of His living community. His disciples certainly were not a 'club' of like-minded people but an aggregation of distinct, wildly contrasting, made-in-God's-image, individuals, some with strong personalities, and others who were natural enemies. Shockingly, *that* is what God calls us to. The development of the Christian community, of believers fellowshipping in communion together, was never intended to be homogeneous.

Evangelism implications

There are several aspects to the relationship categories that have implications regarding evangelism, as we have seen. First, and foremost, we must recognise the work of the Holy Spirit in His convicting and convincing of sin, the need for repentance, and of a restored relationship with God. We cannot work at that level; it is His prerogative. The best we can do within our culture and relational circumstances is proclaim God's Gospel truth and to be witnesses as to what God has done in our lives.

Second, in terms of our responsibility to be proclaimers and witnesses, the relationship structures in each category have implications as far as who defines truth and from whom we are most likely to accept something as being true and reliable (the

---

[7] Brookes, 2019, p. 35

psycho-epistemological priorities we mentioned). These issues will govern the receptiveness, at a human responsibility level, to any claims we may make. For each of the categories, then, and to recap:

1. Individuals: Truth often resides with the postmodern individual. The, 'what's true for you may be true for me…or not.'

2. Societies: Truth is defined by the leadership and vision and mission of the organisation or business, etc., so much may depend on one's rank in the leadership hierarchy.

3. Collectives: If one is seen as an outgrouper, then there may be limited trust in what one might be trying to communicate. It is possible, however, to become a part of the ingroup, though on the periphery, and be trusted more.

4. Communes: Given the close-knit nature of communes consisting of people with very closely linked beliefs, it may be unlikely that a Christian could be a part of a non-Christian commune. Changing beliefs and assumptions from within such a group would take a considerable time, but it is not impossible.

5. Community: The friendship relationships that exist within a grouping of people who simply share a common interest, perhaps a hobby, or just a group of friends, obviously, greatly facilitate sharing, and there should be a greater willingness to accept the beliefs of others when not imposed.

The 'sticking point' in each of these is the creation of shared meaning. For postmodern individuals, this is difficult, and for societies, collectives and communes, meaning is created and defined usually by entities within these, such as the leadership. However, if it were possible to create genuine communities, as we are defining them, these would provide an ideal situation for creating meaning together. This has always been important, but in the 21st-century is even more so. The biblical and theological terms that were well known in prior centuries when church attendance was more common are now unknown or poorly defined by most.

Courses in personal evangelism often have relied on texts from Scripture and concepts that are very meaningful to Christians but may make no sense to non-Christians. Take, as an older example, the much-used "The Four Spiritual Laws". This has been used many, many times in witnessing and no doubt many have found Christ through its use as the Holy Spirit has used it to open hearts. Looking at the first 'law' in its summary form, however, we can see why many non-Christians may have rejected the message.

God loves you and created you to know Him personally.

God's Love: "God so loved the world, that He gave His only begotten Son, that whoever believes in Him should not perish, but have eternal life" (John 3:16).

God's Plan: "Now this is eternal life: that they may know you, the only true God, and Jesus Christ, whom you have sent" (John 17:3, NIV). What prevents us from knowing God personally?

From the very first word, there are problems. Who is God? Given the world's population, there are probably over eight billion definitions floating around! Each of us has an 'image' of God that has been developed over the years and for Christians we hope that this image corresponds to the God of the Bible—though no doubt we know of many instances of those who claim to be Christians but seem to have a very different image. Yet, A. W. Tozer famously wrote: "What comes into our minds when we think about God is the most important thing about us."[8] What 'image' of God does the non-Christian have? Whatever it is, we can almost guarantee that it is not accurate. So, if the first word in the 'spiritual law' has a different meaning, then the rest of the sentence will have a different meaning . . . and so on. The first claim will not make any sense, for example, if the person has an image of God as a monstrous, angry tyrant. Perhaps the other person has an image of God that is at an extreme of being totally loving and indulgent. In that case, the verse from John makes little sense, for why would there be a need for sacrifice? Of course, there are any number of other difficulties with words such as eternal, Son, belief, sin, and so on.

The idea of developing shared meaning in community implies working on these definitions, but this is different from simply saying, "This is what it means!" The other person needs to be drawn into a new meaning for terms and concepts with which they would already be familiar, but with a different meaning. Normally, when speaking of developing meaning in a community, community members have input into the evolving meaning till all agree. In the case of witnessing, the true meaning of the terms may be presumed to be not available for negotiation. Obviously, it is hoped that the one witnessing will not come to have the meaning that belonged to the other!

Teaching and learning within Christian groups

Within any grouping of human beings, incidentally or directed, structured or *ad hoc*, learning will take place. It may be across the group, but it will always be at an individual level as well. Teaching and learning situations for Christians are under the recognition that God owns all truth and that He has given us the capacity to unhide it.[9] This means that learning together, the creation of meaning together and with Him, whether of some biblical principle or a physics equation, points us to God together. As opposed to the

---

[8] Tozer, 1961, p. 1
[9] Beech, 2015

Enemy's lies, which often appear as distortions of God's truth, "We need knowledge that generates wisdom, culminating in adoration of the only wise God."[10]

In order to see learning and meaning creation develop in a community, many different methods may be used, especially as different cultures use different methods. This is a very large and complex field, but we may take a couple of examples. In oral cultures, stories containing important information are told and retold often, so that the material becomes indelibly imprinted on the listeners' memories—"on the village mind"[11] as it were. In collectivist and communalist cultures in particular, importance is given in this process to the ancestors, or those who have gone before, and their wisdom. We see this repeatedly in the New Testament with constant references to those living in Old Testament times. The significance of this in any long-term grouping of people is so important and if there is a break in the chain, then problems quickly arise: *"After that whole generation had been gathered to their fathers, another generation grew up, who knew neither the Lord nor what he had done for Israel"* *(Judges 2:10).*

It is not good enough just to have a textbook or documents (the Israelites had their documents). It requires a relational, cultural transmission . . . in community. This teaching and learning aims for holistic formation and not simply the transmission of information. Writing concerning Bonhoeffer's *Living Together*, David Smith wrote:

> Both the content and the context of the book imply at least three claims about Christian learning: that it involves formation rather than merely information; that this formation arises within shared communal practice and not simply through reflection on ideas; and that the formation process unfolds over time rather than being grasped or mastered in a single act of understanding.[12]

Many, if not all, of our society-based institutions and organisations, of all varieties, actually are founded on teaching and learning. Either the group of people has been brought together specifically for the purpose of teaching and learning, such as in schools and colleges, or some degree of learning is involved in the incorporation into the group in order to achieve the purposes of the group. 'Indoctrination' into any group, community, or communal mindset, obviously, must be done with great care, under Jesus-led, servant leadership, and be guided with reference to God's will and His word. Once thoroughly incorporated into the group, individual mindsets may prove to be strongly resistant to change, so it behoves us to guard the truth. There is much 'fake news' that surrounds us and: "People can maintain an unshakable faith in any proposition, however absurd, when they are sustained by a community of like-minded

---

[10] Bartholomew, 2017, p. 146
[11] Wright, 2015, p. 135
[12] Smith, 2017, para. 13

believers."[13] George Orwell illustrated this, and also the problem of rules becoming more important than relationships in his book, *1984*, where we see lies being portrayed as truth, indeed, all recorded past history needing to be changed constantly to fit with current versions of truth. This is not a post-modern relativism where what is true for you may be true for you but not necessarily for me. In the dystopian, autocratic society that Orwell depicts, there is no relativism. If the state says it is true, it is true—even if the state declares in its motto: "War is peace; Freedom is slavery; Ignorance is strength."[14] Truth and knowledge, therefore, in this case, are redefined for the society's purposes, which are defined by the State.

We not only exist as individuals and as members of groups of one type or another, but we also exist as citizens of countries. We may read Orwell's *1984* as an extrapolation of the wrongs in some cultures we may see around the world today. We see this, however, through the glasses, as it were, that have been prepared for us by our own family, education, peer interactions, and media consumption, which are all influenced by those 'in charge' in some way. These may be leaders in education systems, denominations, or other influencers, but governments, by their power, have a very significant role to play as well. To take a perhaps extreme example of the 'glasses', it may be easy for many in the West to make the claim that those in communist countries have been brainwashed into their belief system, and we can list the errors of their ways. At the same time, however, many in communist countries would no doubt claim that those in the West have been brainwashed by their governments into their belief system and could list the errors of Western beliefs and practices. And each would claim to have the truth and be right. As we move down the quantitative scale, we see the same situation with, for example, political parties, denominations, local churches or schools, to individuals. We cling obsessively to our belief that we are right, however, and most people treat arguments as zero-sum events where one (*I*) is right, and the other (*'opponent'*) is wrong, rather than both emerging with points and learning from the other.

Construction costs

With the aid of the Holy Spirit, then, we can work towards community. Meryn Callander summarised four stages in the development of a community that was originally developed by M. Scott Peck in *A Different Drum*. The first is a pseudo-community built on conflict avoidance. There is no complete openness between members; differences are minimised or ignored, disagreements are avoided, and the aim is the smooth and harmonious functioning of the group. The second stage is chaos. The chaos ensues as well-intentioned group members attempt to remove individual

---

[13] Kahneman, 2015, p. 217
[14] Orwell, 1949, p. 5

differences—to heal and convert, as it were. Any 'leaders' at this stage may be replaced and attempts made, though generally futile, to 'organise' relationships into harmony. The third stage that is identified is one of 'emptiness'. At this stage, group members know each other better, and there is more open communication. "The stage of emptiness is ushered in as members begin to share their own brokenness—their defeats, failures, fears, rather than acting as if they 'have it all together'." [15] The final stage, according to Callander, is one of true community, as group members accept the dark as well as the light side of each other's lives. This requires an identity cost: "The transformation of the group from a collection of individuals into true community requires little deaths in many of the individuals."[16] From this self-sacrifice, healing begins, and true community is birthed. From his experience in the establishment of a Christian community, or commune, in Nazi Germany, Dietrich Bonhoeffer explained that **communal** communities must not be born out of wishful thinking but a commitment to personal cost.

> Innumerable times a whole Christian community has broken down because it has sprung from a wish dream. The serious Christian, set down for the first time in a Christian community, is likely to bring with him a very definite idea of what Christian life together should be and to try to realize it. But God's grace speedily shatters such dreams. Just as surely as God desires to lead us to a knowledge of genuine Christian fellowship, so surely must we be overwhelmed by a great disillusionment with others, with Christians in general, and, if we are fortunate, with ourselves.

> By sheer grace, God will not permit us to live even for a brief period in a dream world. He does not abandon us to those rapacious experiences and lofty moods that come over us like a dream. God is not a God of the emotions but the God of truth. Only that fellowship which faces such disillusionment, with all its unhappy and ugly aspects, begins to be what it should be in God's sight, begins to grasp in faith the promise that is given to it. The sooner this shock of disillusionment comes to an individual and to a community the better for both. A community which cannot bear and cannot survive such a crisis, which insists upon keeping its illusion when it should be shattered, permanently, loses in that moment the promise of Christian community. Sooner or later it will collapse. Every human wish dream that is injected into the Christian community is a hinderance to genuine community and must be banished if genuine community is to survive. He who loves his dream of community more than the Christian community itself becomes a destroyer of the latter, even

---

[15] Callander, 1990, para. 4
[16] Ibid., para. 5

though his personal intentions may be ever so honest and earnest and sacrificial.[17]

Summarizing the difficulties

The title of this book is *The Elusive Ideal of Community*, so why is it so elusive for us? Through the book, many responses to this question have been given, but at this point, it may be useful to summarise some of them in dot-point form.

- Communities, under the definition we are using here, are voluntary groupings of people. We cannot force people to become a community.
- Community members share something or things in common, so the commonality must first be found.
- Community members can be, or become, judgmental and any perceived 'Simon the Zealot' or 'Judas Iscariot' will be sidelined or expelled—often antagonising any friends in the group they may have.
- In a Christian community, members are expected (commanded) to love each other and not just 'get along together'.
- The idea of a community's initiation must never be based only on someone's dream.
- Those initiating the community may have the wrong motives for doing so.
- There will often (usually) be within a community group, someone (or ones) who desire leadership, power or control.
- Developing a community requires a time commitment that many may be unwilling to give.
- Community members may be unwilling to be open and share, to be vulnerable and accountable.
- As a sense of community grows, some, many, or all of the community members may feel that they are not willing to pay the identity cost of membership.
- There may be misunderstandings regarding the nature of 'community' and members may believe, consciously or unconsciously, that they are in a different relationship category and try to act accordingly.
- There may be some who will 'grandstand', proclaiming a moral superiority but using zero-sum arguments with a declared winner and loser.
- 'Personality clashes' or ideological differences between community members often exist. These may be concerning the things purportedly held in common, but they are quite likely to be concerning things outside the community (e.g., differences of political opinion).

---

[17] Bonhoeffer, 1954, pp. 26–27

138

- The community may be infiltrated by some who do not share the common things around which the community was formed. These may simply try to join or the community may desire to grow and invite them in without realising the consequences.
- The love of the idea of community can come to take precedence over the love for others.
- The feeling may grow that leadership, direction, rules and regulations are required, and the community may devolve into a society or organisation.
- The depth of individualism in many people can make open participation in a community difficult, especially as many will inhabit cities and not villages.
- While not inhibiting the initiation of community, for the above reasons, many communities are short-lived.

Where to from here?

Nicky Gumbel, founder of the Alpha movement, was asked why he thought Alpha had become such a phenomenal success worldwide. His response was, "One thing I think, is the genuine community. There's food, people are welcomed, it's non-confrontational, everyone's loved for who they are."[18] As Christians, we may be said to belong to two types of what he terms constitutive communities: *creational* (sharing as God-created beings), and *redemptive* (sharing as those redeemed through Christ). But, as Gumbel noted, we are also called to membership of *expressive* communities, where the fruit of the Spirit, including *agape*, giving, and altruistic love, is expressed to others.

Apart from the 'cost' of *agape* loving and being willing to be loved, when new members are brought into a group—voluntarily, or by invitation—those new members must pay an identity cost in order to conform to the group. In addition, because the new members are individuals and as such will not conform or merge completely into some common identity, the group's nature will change by a small amount, and all other members of the group will therefore also have to pay an identity cost. Obviously, where the group is large, the change may be almost imperceptible, but if the group is small, the cost may be deemed to be too high. Of course, this is why some groups prefer to remain closed to new members. At a national scale, we see the difficulties related to migration, where countries fear a significant change of identity if very large numbers of migrants are admitted. Christian schools have this issue with regard to the admission of students from non-Christian families, and churches can change in character and may even split or dissolve if there is an influx of those who do not fully integrate.

Given the potential for disrupted relationships, in order to negate unwanted change, those administering or leading organised, societal groups of people may access

---

[18] Sheridan, 2019, paras. 35–36

literature and learn by experience the things most likely to promote at least some sense of community or communality—whether this is done in a societal way out of obligation, or genuine caring. One key feature is the acting out of beliefs-in-common. "The *practices* of the community are all important. The very fact that we call them by that name gives a hint: these are the things through which the community *practices* the habits of mind and heart which develop . . . corporate virtues."[19] Bible reading, prayer, and sharing are often incorporated into the practices of sociating Christians intent on developing a sense of togetherness. These may function at different levels as meaning is developed together, values are shared and adopted by members, and in worship in particular, as the Holy Spirit works to encourage His fruit to develop. Other activities and actions that may be taken include commensalism (the sharing in fellowship over a meal as mentioned with regard to the early Church), camps, sports, and other 'team' activities, as well as through the promulgation of values, beliefs, vision and mission. Yonker, Pendery, Klein and Witte[20] also found that thanking and praying for others increased prosocial attitudes and tendencies, which helped build a sense of community. All of these practices are particularly important for young people who seek a coherent 'story' with which to engage and within which to find themselves embedded. While the activities mentioned may encourage positive interpersonal engagement and facilitate meaning creation and maintenance, they fall far short of the born-into, long-term enculturation inherent in communality. And, as Stuart Fowler has seen, all too often, the creation of 'community' becomes merely "something that a group of individuals creates by appropriately organised human activities."[21] Just the same, the sense of long-term communality is encouraged through attempts to immerse participants in a coherent narrative of long standing—the history, norms, and traditions of the institution or group. Church anniversaries have their place! Bellah uses the term 'community' to describe this:

> Communities, in the sense in which we are using the term, have a history—in an important sense they are constituted by their past—and for this reason we can speak of a real community as a "community of memory", one that does not forget its past. In order not to forget that past, a community is involved in retelling its story, its constitutive narrative, and in so doing, it offers examples of the men and women who have embodied and exemplified the meaning of community. These stories of collective history and exemplary individuals are an important part of the tradition that is so central to a community of memory.[22]

---

[19] Wright, 2012, p. 278
[20] Yonker, Pendery, Klein & Witte, 2019
[21] Fowler, 1993, p. 26
[22] Bellah et al, 2008, p. 153

While living on the earth in order to live out God's purposes for us, as part of His story, we are commanded to not do this alone: "We've been created to live in the company of others for a cause much greater than ourselves"[23]: to live in synergistic relationships, and related to God, as exemplified often in the biblical record. This is not for our benefit, nor merely for commanded expressions of love to each other and the world, but because God commands it as a part of His grand design for the cosmos. The other benefits to us and others, while inevitable, are secondary.

Perhaps we are left, then, with an ideal of a *village-like* group that seeks wisdom from those who have gone before, and that trains (disciples) the next generation in all ways pertaining to Godly living. Unlike a theoretical village scenario, this is not a closed knowledge system. Our imminent God is willing and able to add His knowledge for His purposes. This calls us to resist the constant temptation to seek His common grace knowledge for our purposes, or some government's purposes, but to be in tune with God's purposes.

Conclusion

So, the ideal of 'community', or 'Christian community', has proved to be elusive for us. The great difficulty we have in identifying relationship categories or structures is due to the complex, God-given human natures of those we may observe. The categorisation of relationships that we have been using necessarily depends on generalisations and simplifications. For example, to illustrate the level of complexity we face, we might imagine a person in a lunch room at their workplace. They are, by definition, an individual, but they are also a part of the structured 'society' of their workplace. Perhaps they are friendly with the others in the lunch room, a group that likes to eat together and that may be described as a small community. Perhaps there is a clique within the group—a collective—and perhaps there are some who have very close relationships in and out of work time and therefore may act communally. The one person, then, may wear many relational 'hats' at the same time.

It is easy for us to imagine ourselves in different situations and see that we find ourselves functioning relationally in all of the categories in the relationship series around which this book has been based. And it is important to note that the Scriptures do not denounce any of the categories as such, but only their excesses and extremes when taken over by our fallen natures. There is a constant need for empathy, to walk in the shoes of the other person, to pay the price, to be the Good Samaritan, to weep for a Lazarus, and to not judge because of love, or at least for fear of being judged by the same standard (Matthew 7:1–2).

---

[23] Gould, 2019, p. 91

When the idea of a relationship series of categories was first conceived, it was thought that our calling was to be one of moving always from individuality towards communality. Examining the Scriptures and thinking through each of the categories in the series, however, led to the realization that while each has serious failings, given our sinful natures, each has also a biblical foundation, has significant benefits for us, and, to one extent or another, is a part of what it means to be human beings created in the image of the relational God. Created as *individuals* with distinct physical forms, we have at least a degree of what we perceive to be intellectual freedom, and God, by His Holy Spirit, deals with us as individuals. Given the variety of giftedness with which human beings are imbued (c.f., the account of the gifting for the building of the Tabernacle in Exodus), relating pragmatically in structured *societies* has proven to be of mutual benefit and to achieve great things together. Given the natural, biological structure of families, we are also predisposed to *collectivity,* and Scripture calls us to be siblings in God's family collective, with Him at the trusted and honoured head. Scripture also calls us to live in *community*, developing and sharing meaning together. There is also, however, a call to deeper relationships, to communality, and the establishment of *communal* settings within which the next generation may be discipled long-term as communal members.

While human relationality may co-exist in each of the categories in the series, and the ideal is yet to come, it still remains that obviously there must be an allocentrism, an other-centeredness, that is essential when an individual joins any intentional group. This may also be seen in a historical perspective: *faith* regarding what has happened in the past (Christ's substitutionary death and resurrection that binds us together as His Body), *hope* regarding our purposes for living together and the future in Eternity, and *love* for our relationships here and now. Our faith and hope provide commonalities of belief for us to share in communion as Body members in this age, "But the greatest of these is love" (1 Corinthians 13:13).

References

Aboriginal Resource and Development Services. (1998). *The Madayin. Information paper 7.* Author.

Adrono, T. W. (2000). *Introduction to sociology.* Polity Press.

Aldrich, V. C. (1939). An ethics of shame. *Ethics, 50*(1), 57–77.

Anderson, J. (2019). The only metric of success that really matters is the one we ignore. *Quartz.* Retrieved from https://qz.com/1570179/how-to-make-friends-build-a-community-and-create-the-life-you-want/

Angus Reid Institute. (2019). *A portrait of social isolation and loneliness in Canada today.* Author. Retrieved from http://angusreid.org/social-isolation-loneliness-canada/

Archer, M. (2011). *The current crisis: Consequences of neglecting the four key principles of Catholic social doctrine.* Retrieved from https://www.ordosocialis.de/pdf/Archer/The%20current%20crisis.pdf

Archer, M. (2012). The 'Logic of the Gift': Can it find a place within normal economic activity? Retrieved from https://economy.secondspring.co.uk/uploads/articles_19_953760526.pdf

Aristotle, & Brown, L. (Trans.). (2009). *The Nichomachean ethics.* Oxford University Press.

Augustine, & Chadwick, H. (Trans.). (1991). *Saint Augustine: Confessions. A new translation by Henry Chadwick.* Oxford University Press.

Augustine, & Dods, M. (Ed.). (1871). *The works of Aurelius Augustine, Bishop of Hippo: The city of God, Volume 1.* T. & T. Clarke.

Bahovec, I. (2015). Christianity in confrontation with individualism and crisis of Western culture: person, community, dialog, reflexivity, and relationship ethics. *Bogoslovni vestnik, 75*(2), 335–346.

Bailey, K. E. (1991). Informal controlled oral tradition and the Synoptic Gospels. *Asia Journal of Theology, 5*(1), 34–54.

Bartholomew, C. G. (2017). *Contours of the Kuyperian tradition: A systematic introduction.* IVP Academic.

Bartholomew, C., & Goheen, M. W. (2014). *The drama of Scripture: Finding our place in the biblical story.* SPCK.

Bass, A. (2018). Radical and restorationist: Stone-Campbell resources for Christian intentional community. *Missio Dei: A Journal of Missional Theology and Praxis, 9*(2). Retrieved from http://missiodeijournal.com/issues/md-9-2/authors/md-9-2-bass.

Bass, B. M. (1960). *Leadership, psychology, and organizational behavior.* New York: Harper & Row.

Bass, D. B. (2004). *The practicing congregation: Imagining a new old church.* Alban Institute.

Bauman, Z. (2018). *Liquid modernity.* Polity Press.

Bavinck, H. (2004). *Reformed dogmatics: Volume 2: God and Creation.* Baker Academic.

Bavinck, H., & Kloosterman, N. D. (Trans.). (2012). *The Christian family.* Christian's Library Press.

Beech, G. R. (2011). *A study of affective domain factors influencing the decisions of leaders with different cultural perspectives* (Unpublished doctoral thesis, Australian Catholic University). Retrieved from https://doi.org/10.4226/66/5a960c71c6846

Beech, G. R., & Beech, E. G. (2018). A redefinition of leadership: What on earth did we think we were doing? *Christian Teachers Journal, 26*(1), 8–11.

Beilmann, M., & Realo, A. (2012). Individualism-collectivism and social capital at the individual level. *TRAMES, 15*(3), 205–217.

Bell, D. (2016). Communitarianism. In E. N. Zalta (Ed.), *The Stanford Encyclopedia of Philosophy.* Retrieved from https://plato.stanford.edu/archives/sum2016/entries/communitarianism/.

Bellah, R. N., Madsen, R., Sullivan, W. M., Swidler, A., & Tipton, S. M. (2008). *Habits of the heart: Individualism and commitment in American life.* University of California Press.

Benedict, R. (1946). *The chrysanthemum and the sword.* Houghton Mifflin.

Berry, W. (1994). *Health is membership.* Retrieved from http://home.btconnect.com/tipiglen/berryhealth.html.

Bessenecker, S. A. (2006). *The new Friars: The emerging movement serving the world's poor.* InterVarsity Press.

Bettelheim, B. (1979). *The informed heart: Autonomy in a mass age.* Avon Books.

Bird-David, N. (1999). "Animism" revisited: Personhood, environment, and relational epistemology. *Current Anthropology, 40,* 67–91.

Blankenberg, N. (1999). In search of a real freedom: Ubuntu and the media. *Critical Arts, 13*(2), 42–65.

Blaschke, R. C. (2001). *Quest for power: Guidelines for communicating the gospel to animists.* Guardian Books.

Bonhoeffer, D. (1995). Letter to Karl-Friedrich Bonhoeffer (January 14, 1935). In G. B. Kelly & F. B. Nelson (Eds.), *A Testament of freedom: The essential writings of Dietrich Bonhoeffer.* Harper Collins.

Bonhoeffer, D. (1954). *Life together.* Harper & Row.

Bonhoeffer, D., & Green, C. J. (2009). *Sanctorum communio: A theological study of the sociology of the church.* Fortress Press.

Bourdieu, P. (2011). The forms of capital. In I. Szeman & T. Kaposy (Eds.), *Cultural theory: An anthology* (pp. 81–93). Wiley-Blackwell.

Boykin, A. W., Jagers, R. J., & Ellison, C. M. (1997). Conceptualization and measurement of an Afrocultural social orientation. *Journal of Black Studies, 27*(3), 409–418.

Brockhaus, H. (2020). Pope Francis warns Catholics that individualism is 'illusory'. Retrieved from https://www.catholicnewsagency.com/news/pope-francis-warns-catholics-that-individualism-is-illusory-33854.

Brookes, D. (2019). *The second mountain: The quest for a moral life.* Random House.

Buber, M., & Smith, R. G. (2018). *I and thou.* Bloomsbury Academic.

Buttery, E. A., & Wong, Y. H. (1999), The development of a guanxi framework. *Marketing Intelligence & Planning. 17*(3) 147-54.

Callander, M. G. (1990). *Four stages of community.* Retrieved from http://atlc.org/members/resources/four_stages_community.html

Calvin, J., & Beveridge, H. (2008). *Institutes of the Christian religion.* Hendrickson Publishers.

Cepeda, J. H. (2017). The problem of being in Latin America: Approaching the Latin American ontological *sentipensar*. *Journal of World Philosophies, 2, 12–27.*

Chablis, C. F., Heck, P., R., Mandart, J., Benjemin, D. J., & Simons, D. J. (2019). No evidence that experiencing physical warmth promotes interpersonal warmth: Two failures to replicate Williams and Bargh (2008). *Social Psychology, 50*(2), 127–132.

Chiao, J. Y., & Blizinsky, K. D. (2010). Culture-gene coevolution of individualism-collectivism and the serotonin transporter gene. *Proceedings of the Royal Society B, 277,* 529–537.

Cicero, & Shukburgh, S. H. (Trans.). (2009). *The letters and treaties of Cicero and Pliny* (Vol. IX). Cosimo.

Cigna. (2020). Loneliness is at epidemic levels in America. Retrieved from https://www.multivu.com/players/English/8294451-cigna-us-loneliness-survey/docs/IndexReport_1524069371598-173525450.pdf

Cohen, D. (2003). The American national conversation about (everything but) shame. *Social Research, 70*(4), 1075–1108.

Colzato, L. S., van Beest, I., van den Wildenberg, W. P. M. et al. (2010), God: Do I have your attention. *Cognition, 117*(1), 87–94. Retrieved from http://www.psych.utoronto.ca/users/ferber/teaching/visualattention/readings/Oct6/2010ColzatoCognition.pdf

Commonwealth of Australia. (1998). *Northern Territory: Prime Minister's visit. The Senate Adjournment Speech.* Author. Retrieved from http://parlinfo.aph.gov.au:80/parlInfo/genpdf/chamber/hansards/1998-03-25/0163/hansard_frag.pdf;fileType%3Dapplication%2Fpdf

Cooke, M. (1990). *Seeing Yolngu, seeing mathematics.* Batchelor College.

Daffin, L., Tyler, K. M., et al. (2008). Cultural discontinuity: Toward a quantitative investigation of a major hypothesis in education. *Educational Researcher, 37*(5), 280–297.

De Crèvecoeur, J. H. St. J., & Moore, D. D. (2013). *Letters from an American farmer and other essays.* Belknap Press of Harvard University.

Dekar, P. R. (2007). Practices of an Australian Baptist intentional community: Holy Transfiguration Monastery. *Cistercian Studies Quarterly, 44*(4), 377–401.

Dekar, P. R. (2008). *Community of the Transfiguration: The journey of a new monastic community.* Cascade Books.

De Souza, R. J. (2019). Jean Vanier's human communities. *Convivium.* Retrieved from https://www.convivium.ca/articles/jean-vaniers-human-communities

Dietterich, I. (2012). *Twelve marks of New Monasticism.* Retrieved from https://centerforparishdevelopment.wordpress.com/2012/01/16/twelve_marks/

diZereaa, G. (2011). Emergent systems and methodological individualism, Part II: The issue of moral individualism. *Studies in Emergent Order.* Retrieved from https://studiesinemergentorder.org/2011/02/24/emergent-systems-and-methodological-individualism-part-11-the-issue-of-moral-standing/

Donati, P., & Archer, M. S. (2015). *The relational subject.* Cambridge: Cambridge Univ. Press.

Drakulic, S. (1993): *The Balkan Express: Fragments from the other side of the war.* Norton.

Dreher, R. (2018). *The Benedict option: A strategy for Christians in a post-Christian nation.* Sentinel.

Ducharme, J. (2018). Young Americans are the loneliest, according to a new study. *Time*, (May 1, 2018). Retrieved from https://time.com/5261181/young-americans-are-lonely/

Dumas, A. (1993). *The three musketeers*. Wordsworth Editions.

Dumont, L. (2004). *Essays on individualism: Modern ideology in anthropological perspective*. UMI Books on Demand.

Dutton, M. L. (2010). Introduction. In Aelred of Rievaulx, L. C. Braceland, (Trans.), & M; L. Dutton (Ed.). (2010). *Spiritual friendship* (pp. 13–50). Cistercian Publications.

Eberstadt, M. (2003). *How the West really lost God*. Templeton Press.

Eliot, T. S. (1940). *The idea of a Christian society*. Faber & Faber.

Escobar, A. (2016). Sentipensar con la tierra: Las luchas territoriales y la dimension ontológica de las epistemologías del Sur. *Revista de Antropología Iberoamericana, 11*(1), 11–32.

Fowler, S. (1993). Communities, organizations, and people. *Pro Rege, 21*(4), 20–32.

Fowler, S. (2004). Experiencing community in the school. In J. Ireland, R. Edlin, K. Dickens (Eds.), *Pointing the way: Directions for Christian education in the new millennium* (pp. 115–130). National Institute for Christian Education.

Gadamer, H-G. (2014). *Truth and method*. Bloomsbury Academic.

Gambrel, P. A., & Cianci, R. (2003). Maslow's Hierarchy of Needs: Does it apply in a collectivist culture? *Journal of Applied Management and Entrepreneurship, 8*(2), 143–161.

Gates, W. (2018). What I learned at work this year. *Gates Notes: The Blog of Bill Gates*. Retrieved from https://www.gatesnotes.com/About-Bill-Gates/Year-in-Review-2018.

Geertz, C. (1983). Local knowledge: Fact and law in comparative perspective. In *Local knowledge: Further essays in interpretive anthropology* (pp. 167–234). Basic Books.

Gegeo, D. W., & Watson-Gegeo, K. A. (2001). "How we know": Kwara'ae rural villagers doing indigenous epistemology. The Contemporary Pacific, 3(1), 55–88.

Girard, R. & Freccero, Y. (Trans.). (1986). The scapegoat. Harvard University Press.

Gold, T., Guthrie, D., & Wank, D. (Eds.). (2002). Social connections in China: Institutions, culture, and the changing nature of guanxi. Cambridge University Press.

Gould, P. M. (2019). *The outrageous idea of the missional professor: International edition*. Culture and Science Publishers.

Grayman-Simpson, N., & Mattis, J. S. (2017). Communalism scale cultural validity study. Africology: *The Journal of Pan African Studies, 10*(3), 127–135.

Hailey, J. (2008). *Ubuntu: A literature review*. A paper prepared for the Tutu Foundation. Retrieved from http://citeseerx.ist.psu.edu/viewdoc/download?doi=10.1.1.459.6489&rep=rep1&type=pdf

Harinam, V., & Henderson, R. (2019). What doesn't kill us brings us together. *Quillette*, April 7, 2019. Retrieved from https://quillette.com/2019/04/07/what-doesnt-kill-us-brings-us-together/

Harris, N., Walgrave, L., & Braithwaite, J. (2004). Emotional dynamics in restorative conferences, *Theoretical criminology, 8*(1), 191–210.

Hart, P. (2006). *A monastic vision for the 21st century: Where do we go from here?* Cistercian Publications.

Hegeman, B. (2006). *The four hidden faces of our deepest cultural values: The proposal of a missiological rubric for inner and cultural values.* Unpublished PhD thesis.

Helfferich, T. (2009). *Thirty Years' War: A documentary history.* Hackett Publishing.

Higgs, P. (2010). Towards an indigenous African epistemology of community in education research. *Procedia Social and Behavioral Sciences, 2*(2010), 2414–2421.

Hobbes, T., & Stanlick, N. A. (2016). *The essential leviathan: A modernized edition.* Hackett Publishing Company.

Hofstede, G. (1984). *Culture's consequences: International differences in work-related values.* Sage Publications, Inc.

Hofstede, G., Hofstede, G. J., & Minkov, M. (2017). *Cultures and organizations: Software of the mind: intercultural cooperation and its importance for survival.* MTM.

Homik, H. J. (2010). Old world monasteries for new generations. In R. B. Kruschwitz (Ed.). *Monasticism old and new* (pp. 53–59). Baylor University.

House, R. J., Hanges, P. J., Javidan, M., Dorfman, P. W., & Gupta, V., (Eds.). (2004). *Culture, leadership, and organizations: The GLOBE study of 62 societies.* Sage.

Huff, L. C., & Kelley, L. (2003). Levels of organizational trust in individualist versus collectivist societies: A seven-nation study. *Organizational Science, 14*(1), 81–90.

Ijzerman, H., & Semin, G. R. (2009). The thermometer of social relations: Mapping social proximity on temperature. *Psychological Science, 20*(10), 1214–1220.

Irvine, J. (2018, June 24). It takes a village to raise a child but the village is missing. *The Sydney Morning Herald.* Retrieved from https://www.smh.com.au/business/the-economy/it-takes-a-village-to-raise-a-child-but-the-village-is-missing-20180624-p4zned.html

Jagers, R. J., & Mock, L. O. (1995). The Communalism Scale and collectivistic-individualistic tendencies: Some preliminary findings. *Journal of Black Psychology, 21*(2), 153–167.

Jobes, K. H. (2009). *1 Peter.* Grand Rapids, MI: Baker Academic.

Junger, S. (2016). *Tribe: On homecoming and belonging.* Hatchette Book Group.

Jüri, A., & Anu, R. (2004). Individualism-collectivism and social capital. *Journal of Cross-Cultural Psychology, 35*(1), 29–49.

Kaemingk, M. (2018). *Christian hospitality and Muslim immigration in an age of fear.* Eerdmans.

Kahneman, D. (2015). *Thinking, fast and slow.* Farrar, Straus and Giroux.

Kaplan, S. (2020). What is community?: An illustration. *Comment, 38*(1), 72–74. Retrieved from https://www.cardus.ca/comment/article/what-is-community/

Kaufman, I. J. (2010). Evangelicals and monastics. In R. B. Kruschwitz (Ed.). *Monasticism old and new* (pp. 26–32). Baylor University.

Kauka, E. O. (2018). Analysis of the implications of ubuntu metaphysics on educational praxis. *International Journal of Novel Research in Education and Learning, 5*(1), 43–52.

Keesmaat, S. C., & Walsh, B. J. (2019). *Romans disarmed: Resisting empire, demanding justice.* Brazos Press.

Keller, T. (2019, June 25). *Everyone says they want community and deep friendship.* Twitter: https://twitter.com/timkellernyc/status/1143452272015433728?lang=en.

Khan, Z., & Botes, N. (2017). In your hands & self-portrait: Introductory spatial design exercises in the first- year studio. *Proceedings of the 14th National Design Education Forum of Southern Africa Conference* (104–117). Retrieved from http://www.defsa.org.za/papers/your-hands-self-portrait.

Kierkegaard, S., & Lowie, W. (1944). *Attack upon "Christendom".* Princeton University Press.

Kosfeld, M., Heinrichs M., Zak, P. J., Fischbacher, U., & Fehr, E. (2005). Oxytocin Increases trust in humans. *Nature, 435*(2005), 673–676.

Koyzis, D. (2017). *Abraham Kuyper and the pluralist claims of the liberal project, Part 2: The Church as voluntary association.* Retrieved from http://kuyperian.com/abraham-kuyper-pluralist-claims-liberal-project-part-2-church-voluntary-association/

Križan, M. (1997). Communitarianism, Charles Taylor, and the post-Communist transition. *Politicka misao, 34*(5), 152–170.

Kuyper, A., & Bratt, J. D. (Ed.). (1998). *Abraham Kuyper: A centennial reader.* Eerdmans.

Kuyper, A., & Jellema, D. (Ed.). (1950). *Christianity and the class struggle.* Piet Hein Publishers.

Kuyper, A., Ballor, J. J., Grabill, S. J., Kloosterman, N. D., Van, M. E. M., & Mouw, R. J. (2016). *Common grace: God's gifts for a fallen world.* Lexham Press.

Kwon, M. K., Geetanjali, S., & Rashmi, A. (2015). Who said what: The effects of cultural mindsets on perceptions of endorser–message relatedness. *Journal of Consumer Psychology, 25*(3), 389-403.

Laertius, D., & Yonge, C. D. (Trans). (1853). *The lives and opinions of eminent philosophers.* Henry G. Bohn.

Levin, Y. (2017). *The fractured republic: Renewing America's social contract in the age of individualism.* Basic Books.

Lewis, C. S. (2013). The Screwtape letters (Annotated Edition). HarperOne.

Lieberman, M. D. (2015). *Social—why our brains are wired to connect.* Oxford University Press.

Locke, J., & Peardon, T. P. (1997). *The second treatise of government.* Prentice Hall.

Lonner, W., & Berry, W. (Eds.). (1994). Introduction. In U. Kim, H. Triandis, C. Kagitcibasi, S. Choi, & G. Yoon (Eds.), *Individualism and collectivism: Theory, method, and applications* (p. xv). Sage.

Leung, T. K. P., & Wong, Y. H (2001). The ethics and positioning of guanxi in China. *Marketing Intelligence & Planning, 19*(1), 55–64.

Lou, S., & Han, S. (2014). The association between an oxytocin receptor gene polymorphism and cultural orientations. *Culture and Brain, 2*(1), 89–107. Retrieved from https://link.springer.com/content/pdf/10.1007/s40167-014-0017-5.pdf

Lui, P. P., & Rollock, D. (2018). Greater than the sum of its parts: Development of a measure of collectivism among Asians. *Cultural Diversity and Ethnic Minority Psychology, 24*(2), 242–259.

Machan, T. R. (2016). Individualism in the right key. *Contemporary Readings in Law and Social Justice, 8*(1), 11–19.

MacIntyre, A. (2017). *After virtue: A study in moral theory* (3rd ed.). University of Notre Dame Press.

Maendel, E. (2019). *Life in community: The three dangers of community living.* Retrieved from https://www.bruderhof.com/en/voices-blog/life-in-community/the-three-dangers-of-community-living

Maluleke, T. (1999). The misuse of 'ubuntu.' *Challenge, 53,* 12–13.

Man, C. F., & Cheng, C. Y (1996). *The Chinese guanxiology.* Institute of Asian Pacific Studies, Chinese University of Hong Kong.

Marinov, B. (2018). The destructive nature of collectivism. *Axe to the Root Podcast: Episode 76.* War Room Productions. Retrieved from https://reconstructionistradio.com/the-destructive-nature-of-collectivism/

Marx, K. (1943). On the Jewish question. In R. Tucker (Ed.), *The Marx-Engels reader* (pp. 26–46). Norton & Company.

Maslow, A. (1970). *Motivation and personality.* New York: Harper & Row.

McCullock, G. (2019). *Because Internet: Understanding the new rules of language.* Riverhead Books.

Mentiki, I. (1984). Person and community in African traditional thought. In R. A. Wright (Ed.), *African philosophy* (3rd ed., pp. 171–182). University Press of America.

Metz, T. (2017), Replacing development: An Afro-communal approach to global justice. *Philosophical Papers, 46*(1), 111–137.

Miller, B. (2015). Why (some) knowledge is the property of a community and possibly none of its members. *The Philosophical Quarterly, 65*(260), 417–441. Retrieved from https://academic.oup.com/pq/article-abstract/65/260/417/1546776/

Mirkmayer, U., & Ruggeri, D. (2015). Make it real. Make it matter. Make it last. *Focus, 11,* 26–38. Retrieved from https://digitalcommons.calpoly.edu/cgi/viewcontent.cgi?referer=&httpsredir=1&article=1282&context=focus

Mnyaka, M., & Motlhabi, M. (2005). The African concept of Ubuntu/Botho and its socio-moral significance. *Black Theology, 3,* 215–237.

Moemeka, A. A. (1998). Communalism as a fundamental dimension of culture. *Journal of Communication, 48*(4), 118–141.

Mourey, J. A., Oyserman, D., & Yoon, C. (2013). One without the other: Seeing relationships in everyday objects. *Psychological Science, 24*(9), 1615–1622.

Mouw, R. J. (2011). *Abraham Kuyper: A short and personal introduction.* William B. Eerdmans.

Muller, R. (2000). *Honor and shame: Unlocking the door.* Xlibris.

Muller, R. (2006). *The messenger, the message and the community: Three critical issues for the cross-cultural church planter.* CanBooks.

Nietzsche, F. (2019). *The will to power.* Place of publication not identified: Dover Publications.

Nietzsche, F. W., Tille, A., & Bozman, M. M. (1958). *Thus spake Zarathustra.* Dent.

Nozaki, W. (2011). The new monasticism: A quest for spiritual renewal in the urban desert. *Christian Research Journal, 34*(3). Retrieved from https://www.equip.org/article/new-monasticism-quest-spiritual-renewal-urban-desert/

Nyasani, P. J. (1989). The ontological significance of "I" and "We" in African philosophy. *I, We and Body, 3*(3),13–26. Retrieved from http://www.galerie-inter.de/kimmerle/frameText8.htm.

Nyathu.N, (2005), *The ubuntu dialogue: Decolonising discourse and dualism in organisation studies.* Unpublished Masters Dissertation, Warwick University.

Oishi, S., & Kisling, J. (2009). The mutual constitution of residential mobility and individualism. In *Understanding culture: Theory, research, and application* (pp. 223–238). Taylor & Francis.

Ong, W. J. (1968). World as view and world as event. *American Anthropologist, 71,* 634–647.

Online Etymological Dictionary. (2001–2018). *Community.* Retrieved from https://www.etymonline.com/word/community#etymonline_v_17249

Orwell, G. (1949). *1984.* Harcourt.

Oviawe, J. O. (2016). How to rediscover the *ubuntu* paradigm in education. *International Review of Education, 62,* 1–10.

Oyewum, O. (2016). *The invention of women: Making an African sense of Western gender discourses.* University of Minnesota Press.

Oyserman, D. (2015). *Culture as situated cognition.* Retrieved from https://www.researchgate.net/publication/299881172_Culture_as_Situated_Cognit ion

Oyserman, D., & Yan. V. X. (2019). Making meaning: A culture-as- situated cognition approach to the consequences of cultural fluency and disfluency. In S. Kitayama & D. Cohen (Eds.), *Handbook of Cultural Psychology* (pp. 536–565). Guilford Press.

Paunov, M. (2019). Social trust as an infrastructure element of cultures. *Advances in Management & Applied Economics, 9*(2), 19–35.

Powell, C. (May 30, 2019). *Four ways to bring community support to your school.* Retrieved from http://blogs.edweek.org/edweek/globallearning/2019/05/fourwaystobringcommunit ysupporttoyourschool.html

Preston, S. G. (2005). *What Is New Monasticism?* Retrieved from http://www.prayerfoundation.org/what_is_new_monasticism.htm

Proffitt, D. (2016). *Convergent commensality: Towards generational reconciliation through differentiated table fellowship.* Doctor of Ministry. Paper 138. George Fox University. Retrieved from http://digitalcommons.georgefox.edu/dmin/138.

Putnam, R. (2000). *Bowling alone.* Simon & Schuster.

Quan-Baffour, K. P., & Romm, N. R. A. (2015). Ubuntu-inspired training of adult literacy teachers as a route to generating "community" enterprises. *Journal of Literacy Research, 46*(4), 455–474.

Relational Schools Foundation. (2019). *Research.* Retrieved from https://relationalschools.org/research/

Rae, M. (2003). Creation and promise: Towards a theology of history. In C. Bartholomew, C. S. Evans, M Healy & M, Rae (Eds.), *"Behind" the text: History and Biblical Interpretation* (pp. 267–299). Zondervan.

Remember Singapore. (September 17, 2013). *Kampong: Spirit and Gotong Royong.* Retrieved from https://remembersingapore.org/2013/09/17/kampong-spirit-and-gotong-royong/

Robinson, S. L. (1996). Trust and the breach of the psychological contract. *Administrative Science Quarterly, 41,* 574–599.

Roth, G. (1978). Introduction. In M. Weber, G. Roth, & C. Wittich, *Economy and society* (pp. xxxiii–cix). University of California Press.

Rousseau, J. J., & Cole, G. D. H. (Trans.). (1762–2016). *The social contract.* CreateSpace Independent Publishing Platform.

Ruch, E., & Anyanwu, K. C. (1984). *African philosophy: An introduction to the main philosophical trends in contemporary Africa.* Catholic Books Agency.

Sacks, J. (2011). *The great partnership: Science, religion, and the search for meaning.* Schocken.

Sawyer, R. K. (2005). *Social emergence: Societies as complex systems.* Cambridge University Press.

Scheff, T. J. (2003). Shame in self and society. *Symbolic Interaction, 26*(2), 239–262.

Schwartz, S. J., Weisskirch, R. S., Hurley, E. A., Zamboanga, B. L., Park, I. J. K., Kim, S. Y., . . . Greene, A. D. (2010). Communalism, familism, and filial piety: Are they birds of a collectivist feather? *Cultural Diversity and Ethnic Minority Psychology, 16*(4), 548–560.

Sedikides, C. (2002). Individual, relational and collective self: Partners, opponents, or strangers? *Advances in Experimental Social Psychology, 48*, 235–295.

Senghor, L. S., & Cook, M. (1968). *On African socialism.* Praeger.

Sergionvanni, T. J. (1994). *Building community in schools.* Jossey-Bass.

Sergiovanni, T. J. (1994). Organizations or communities? Changing the metaphor changes the theory. *Educational Administration Quarterly, 30*(2), 214–226.

Sergiovanni, T. J. (2007). *Rethinking leadership: A collection of articles.* Hawker Brownlow Education.

Shaffer, D. R. (2011). *Social and personality development.* W. Ross MacDonald School, Resource Services Library.

Shenker, B. (1986). *Intentional communities: Ideology and alienation in communal societies.* Routledge.

Sheridan, G. (2019). *Is Christianity making a comeback?* Email newsletter, 8 July, National Alliance of Christian Leaders.

Smith, D. (2009). *Learning from the stranger: Christian faith and cultural diversity.* William B. Eerdmans.

Smith, D. I. (2017). Teaching Bonhoeffer: Pedagogy and peripheral practices. *International Journal of Christianity & Education, 21*(2), 146–159. Retrieved from https://www.researchgate.net/publication/316246593_Teaching_Bonhoeffer_Peda gogy_and_peripheral_practices

Smith, J. K. A. (2014). *How (not) to be secular.* Wm. B. Eerdmans.

Snyder, A. (2020). The tribes that bind. *Comment, 38*(1), 4–9. Retrieved from https://www.cardus.ca/comment/article/the-tribes-that-bind/

Sorokin, P. A. 1957. *Social & cultural dynamics: A study of change in major systems of art, truth, ethics, law and social relationships.* Porter Sargent.

Sosis, R. (2000). Religion and intragroup cooperation: Preliminary results of a comparative analysis of utopian communities. *Cross-Cultural research, 34*(1), 70–87.

South African Government. (1997). *White Paper for social welfare: Principles, guidelines, recommendations, proposed policies and programmes for developmental social welfare in South Africa.* Author.

Sparks, J. (1840). *The works of Benjamin Franklin; containing several political and historical tracts not included in any former edition, and many letters, official and private, not hitherto published; with notes and a life of the author.* Boston: Hillard, Gray & Company. Retrieved from

https://archive.org/stream/sparksbenfrank07jarerich/sparksbenfrank07jarerich_djv
u.txt

Stackhouse, J. G. (2018). *Why you're here: Ethics for the real world*. Oxford University Press.

Studdert, D., & Walkerdine, V. (2016). *Rethinking community research: Inter-relationality, communal being and commonality*. Palgrave Macmillan.

Taylor, C. (1999). Conditions of an unforced consensus on human rights. In J. R. Bauer & D. Bell (Eds.), *The East Asian challenge for human rights*. Cambridge University Press.

Taylor, C. (2002). Gadamer on the Human Sciences. In R. Dostal (Ed.), *The Cambridge companion to Gadamer* (pp. 126–142). Cambridge University Press.

Taylor, C. (2007). *A secular age*. The Belknap Press.

Tedla, E. (1996). *Sankofa: African thought and education*. Peter Lang.

Teresa, & Benenate, B. (2010). *In the heart of the world: Thoughts, stories & prayers*. New World Library.

Tinder, G. (1989). *The political meaning of Christianity: An interpretation*. Louisiana State University Press.

Tönnies, F., & Loomis, C. P. (1957). *Community and society*. Harper Torchbooks.

Toynbee, A. (1947). *A study of history*. Oxford University Press.

Triandis, H. C. (1989). The self and social behavior in differing cultural contexts. *Psychological Review, 96*(3), 506–520.

Triandis, H. C. (1995). *Individualism and collectivism*. Routledge.

Triandis, H. C., Bontempo, R., Villareal, M. J., Asai, M., & Lucca, N. (1988). Individualism and collectivism: Cross-cultural perspectives on self-ingroup relationships. *Journal of Personality and Social Psychology, 54,*323–338.

Trugden, R. (2000). *Why warriors lie down and die*. Aboriginal Resource and Development Services.

Tozer, A. W. (1961). *The knowledge of the holy: The attributes of God, their meaning in the Christian life*. Harper & Row.

Turkle, S. (2015). *Reclaiming conversation; The power of talk in a digital age*. Penguin.

Tutu, D. (1999). *No future without forgiveness*. New York: Doubleday.

Tutu, D. (2004). *God has a dream: A vision of hope for our time*. Doubleday.

Uskul, A. K., Oyserman, D., & Schwarz, N. (2010). Cultural emphasis on honour, modesty or self-enhancement: Implications for the survey response process. To appear in J. Harkness et al. (Eds.), *Survey methods in multinational, multiregional and multicultural contexts* (pp. 191–202). Wiley.

Uslaner, E. M. (2000). Producing and consuming trust, *Political Science Quarterly, 115*(4): 569–590.

Van Der Walt, B. J. (1997). *Afrocentric or Eurocentric*. IRS.

Van der Merwe, W. L. (1996). Philosophical and multi-cultural context of (post)Apartheid South Africa. *Ethical Perspectives, 3*(1), 76–90.

Van Til, K. A. (2008). Subsidiarity and sphere-sovereignty: A match made in . . .? *Theological Studies, 60,* 610–636.

Venter, E. (2004). The notion of Ubuntu and communalism in African educational discourse. *Studies in Philosophy and Education, 23,* 149–160.

Vogt, L., & Laher, S. (2009). The five factor model of personality and individualism/collectivism in South Africa: An exploratory study. *Psychology in Society, 37*, 39–54.

Voltaire, M., & Kneeland, A. (Trans.). (1836). *A Philosophical Dictionary: From the French of M. de Voltaire.* J. Q. Adams.

Vygotsky, L. S. (1987). Thinking and speech. In R. W. Rieber & A. S. Carton (Eds.), *The collected works of L. S. Vygotsky: Vol. 1. Problems of general psychology* (pp. 37–285). Plenum.

Waghid, Y., & Smeyers, P. (2012). Reconsidering Ubuntu: On the educational potential of a particular ethic of care. *Educational Philosophy and Theory, 44* (supplement 2), 6–20.

Waterman, A. S. (1981). Individualism and interdependence. *American Psychologist, 36*(7), 762-773.

Wenger, E. (2018). Communities of practice: Learning as a social system. *Systems Thinker*. Retrieved from https://thesystemsthinker.com/communities-of-practice-learning-as-a-social-system/

Wilson-Hartgrove, J. (2008). *New monasticism: What it has to say to today's church.* Brazos Press.

Wilson-Hartgrove, J. (2010). A vision so old it looks new. In R. B. Kruschwitz (Ed.). *Monasticism old and new* (pp. 11–18). Waco, TX: Baylor University.

Witte, J., Jr. (1999). The biography and biology of liberty: Abraham Kuyper and the American Experiment. *Koers, 2&3*, 173–195.

Wittgenstein, L. (2009). *Philosophical investigations.* Blackwell Publishing.

Wright, N. T. (2012). *After you believe: Why Christian character matters.* HarperCollins.

Wright, N. T. (2015). *Jesus and the victory of God.* SPCK.

Wright, N. T. (2018). The fallen shrine: Lisbon 1755 and the triumph of Epicureanism. *Discerning the dawn: History, eschatology and New Creation* (Lecture 1). St Andrews University. Retrieved from https://www.giffordlectures.org/lectures/discerning-dawn-history-eschatology-and-new-creation.

Wu, J. (2013). *Biblical Theology from a Chinese perspective: Interpreting Scripture through the lens of honor and shame.* Retrieved from http://ojs.globalmissiology.org/index.php/english/article/viewFile/1217/2821

Yau-fai Ho, D. (1976). On the concept of face. *American Journal of Sociology, 81*(4). (Jan., 1976), 867–884.

Yonker, J. E., Pendery, A. R., Klein, C., & Witte. J. (2019). Relational-based Christian practices of gratitude and prayer positively impact Christian university students' reported prosocial tendencies. *International Journal of Christianity & Education, 32*(2), 150–170.

Yūki, M., & Brewer, M. B. (2014). *Culture and group processes.* Oxford University Press.

www.ingramcontent.com/pod-product-compliance
Lightning Source LLC
Chambersburg PA
CBHW070123260726

48658CB00001B/238